HIS
LOVE
ENDURES
FOR EVER

HIS
LOVE
ENDURES
FOR EVER

REFLECTIONS ON
THE LOVE OF GOD

GARRY J. WILLIAMS

INTER-VARSITY PRESS
Norton Street, Nottingham NG7 3HR, England
Email: ivp@ivpbooks.com
Website: www.ivpbooks.com

First published 2015

British Library Cataloguing in Publication Data
A catalogue record for this book is available from the British Library.

ISBN: 978-1-78359-283-8

Set in Monotype Garamond 11/13pt
Typeset in Great Britain by CRB Associates, Potterhanworth, Lincolnshire
Printed and bound in Great Britain by Ashford Colour Press Ltd, Gosport, Hampshire

Inter-Varsity Press publishes Christian books that are true to the Bible and that communicate the gospel, develop discipleship and strengthen the church for its mission in the world.

Inter-Varsity Press is closely linked with the Universities and Colleges Christian Fellowship, a student movement connecting Christian Unions in universities and colleges throughout Great Britain, and a member movement of the International Fellowship of Evangelical Students. Website: www.uccf.org.uk.

In memory of my mother,
Dorothy Anne Williams,
who knew this love.

And for her grandchildren,
Emily, Ben, Alice and Jonathan,
with the prayer that they will abide in it.

CONTENTS

ACKNOWLEDGMENTS

The idea for this book originated in November 2010, when I spoke at a conference in Sheffield for Christ Church, Fulwood. It was the enthusiasm and thoughtful response of the people there that encouraged me to think that the approach taken in the talks might usefully be applied to writing a doctrinal and devotional book on the love of God.

I am very grateful to the Board of London Theological Seminary for the period of study leave in the summer of 2012 during which most of the book was written, and for a further period in 2014 during which it was finished. It is a delight to work in an institution that is sufficiently committed to the ongoing theological growth of its faculty to set them free for study and writing that is not related to preparing the next lecture. In particular, I am grateful to David Green, Nigel Redford and Robert Strivens for taking on the extra burdens involved in looking after the work of the John Owen Centre during my absences.

I first closely studied the doctrine of God's love for a course I team taught in 2001 with David Field and Mike Ovey. I esteem them both as teachers and their lectures have left their mark on this book. The Lord has taken us to different places, but I look forward to the day when we stand together to praise his love.

The bulk of the writing was done in the United States where we were able to live as a family for three months in 2012 due to the generosity of friends old and new. Thank you Luca and Jennie Grillo for lending us your sylvan Amherst home that proved such a conducive environment for work and rest. While in the States we were touched by the kindnesses of many others, some of whom we had not even met before. Thank you Mike and Sue Renihan for the capacious car, Tom and Suzie Oates for the island holiday, and Paul and Christy Wolfe for the Virginian hospitality. During our stay in Massachusetts we greatly appreciated the warm welcome and fellowship at West Springfield Covenant Community Church in Springfield, Massachusetts. It was an apt blessing that while writing about the love of God we were experiencing it in the generosity of his people to us.

Garry J. Williams
Epiphany, 2015

INTRODUCTION

> God is love. In this the love of God was made manifest among
> us, that God sent his only Son into the world, so that we might live
> through him. In this is love, not that we have loved God but that
> he loved us and sent his Son to be the propitiation for our sins.
>
> (1 John 4:8–10)

God is love. There can be few more famous statements in the Bible,
and few more wonderful. Here is a truth that is simple enough for
a small child to grasp and yet deep enough to occupy us for eternity.
Here is the same good news of the gospel of the death of Christ
that is believed by a toddler and yet has kept busy some of the
greatest minds in human history with its unfathomable profundity.
Here is the revelation of the heart of God that grips us when we
first come to know Jesus Christ and holds us to him throughout our
Christian lives. Here is the grace that amazes us because it gives us
what we do not deserve, and keeps giving it.

But here too is a statement like a wax nose that can be bent in
innumerable directions. As Trevor Hart comments, 'simply to repeat
the biblical assertion that "God is love" is certainly not to answer
any significant theological questions'.[1] The idea that God is love is
too readily isolated from its wider biblical context and is twisted.
The temptation is to refashion it 'after our likeness', since we all too
easily make our own human love the definition of God's love. In
the creation God made man in his likeness, but in our rebellion we

---

1. Trevor Hart, 'How Do We Define the Nature of God's Love?', in
Kevin J. Vanhoozer (ed.), *Nothing Greater, Nothing Better: Theological
Essays on the Love of God* (Grand Rapids: Eerdmans, 2001), p. 95.

attempt to make him in ours. Rather than remembering that it is *God* who is love, we presume that the love of God is the *same as* human love, and love – our love – becomes God.

Whole theologies have been built on misunderstandings of this statement, many of them simply reflecting common cultural assumptions about love, as David Wells argues:

> John's sentence defining love would have been completed quite differently in the West today. In this is love, many would say, that God is there for us when we need him. He is there for what we need from him. He is love in that he gives inward comfort and makes us feel better about ourselves. He is love in that he makes us happy, that he gives us a sense of fulfilment, that he gives us stuff, that he heals us, that he does everything to encourage us each and every day.[2]

Given the prominence of such conceptions of love in our culture it is all the more urgent that we discern the true, biblical definition of God's love. Wrong definitions press upon us. I hope that this book will serve as a form of inoculation that will protect you against mistaken accounts of God's love, accounts that flatten out the difference between divine and human love. Nevertheless, because my desire is to leave you filled with wonder at the love of God rather than feeling you have just witnessed a bloody theological bout, I will only occasionally explicitly engage such mistaken theologies along the way. I am convinced that, if we attend to it properly, the biblical doctrine of God's love will itself suffice to expose the false paths we should not follow.

It is particularly easy to define God's love in terms of our own experiences, as distinct from his other attributes. Wells makes this point:

> We assume we know what God's love is because it connects with our experience in a way that many of his other attributes do not. And why is this? The answer, obviously, is that there is no parallel in our experience

---

2. David F. Wells, *God in the Whirlwind: How the Holy-Love of God Reorients Our World* (Nottingham: Inter-Varsity Press, 2014), p. 33.

to many of God's other attributes such as his eternality, omnipresence, omniscience, or omnipotence. But there is to his love.[3]

We use the term 'love' in an incredibly wide range of ways, for everything from parental love to love for jam sandwiches. Most often we take romantic or marital love as our defining model for the love of God. There is strong biblical support for this comparison. Most Christian interpreters have read the relationship in the Song of Songs as a picture of the relationship between Christ and the church. God told the prophet Hosea to take an unfaithful wife in order to illustrate vividly his own relationship to his wayward people (chs. 1–3). Jeremiah depicts Israel as the Lord's unfaithful bride (chs. 2–3) and Ezekiel tells the story of Jerusalem as an abandoned baby nurtured by the Lord and taken as his bride before falling into prostitution (ch. 16). In Ephesians 5:22–33 the apostle Paul points to the love of Christ for the church as a model for the love of a husband for his wife. At the end of the Bible the New Jerusalem comes down from heaven 'prepared as a bride adorned for her husband' (Rev. 21:2). In these and other texts the Bible itself points us to the marriage relationship as a way of grasping something of God's love for the church.

When it speaks like this about God's love, the Bible answers many of our questions about what God is like, but it also raises further questions, and it is in answering these questions that we often go wrong. For example, we more than previous generations know painfully well that human marital love can be fickle and often ends tragically in divorce. So when we read that God loves us as his bride, are we to conclude that he might stop loving us, as a husband might stop loving his wife? Should we fear that, like human marital love, God's love might come and go, and even die? Within the happiest human marriage feelings of love fluctuate, ebbing one day but flowing strongly the next. We can feel full of love, brimming with it, or we can feel cool and detached. Is God like that? Does his love vary in its intensity, perhaps in response to how much we love him? Human love is sometimes more an act of resolve than a passionate

---

3. Ibid., p. 79.

feeling. It can rest more on the memory of a past vow than on a present sensation. What does love mean for God? Is it a decision he has made, or is it a feeling that always burns within him?

Does God even have feelings as we do? What have Christian theologians meant by asserting that he is 'without body, parts or passions'?[4] The idea of an emotionless God might sound unattractive. We might want God to be emotional, to *feel* for us. But perhaps it is not so simple, since not all emotion is good emotion. Imagine a friend tells you about some situation he faced and says, 'I'm afraid I got very emotional about it'; or someone describes a mutual acquaintance as 'always very emotional'. These are not positive statements. 'Being emotional' can be a negative thing. We sometimes find ourselves being irritable and impatient and have no idea why. We find it hard to speak kindly to our children or our colleagues. For some inexplicable reason we feel low. Yesterday we were full of life and energy, but today we have a hollow feeling inside. These are all emotional states. Does God share them? Is his love emotional love? These questions show us that the idea 'God is love' is very unclear if it is considered in artificial isolation, and it needs thoughtful consideration.

The chapters in this book all consist of a doctrinal explanation followed by a meditation on its spiritual significance. The first two chapters are 'method' chapters looking at the problems and possibility of knowing God. Chapter 1 examines the difficulty we have in knowing God as small and sinful creatures. Chapter 2 explores how God has made himself known in his Son, by His Spirit and through the words of the Bible.

Having described the way in which God reveals himself, I turn in the remaining ten chapters to look specifically at what God has revealed of his love. This does mean that the discussion of the love of God itself is delayed until late in chapter 3, but the material in the first two chapters is crucial for shaping the rest. Our understanding of *how* God reveals himself will have a decisive effect on *what* we think he has revealed. For example, if the councils of the church

---

4. A phrase used in both the Thirty-Nine Articles (Article 1) and the Westminster Confession of Faith (2.1).

give us authoritative revelation then its content will be *this*, but if only the Bible is the final authority then it will be *that*. And even if we agree that only the Bible is the authoritative revelation of God, we still need to know how to read it. How we think the Bible works as revelation will affect how we read it. This is why the first two chapters matter even if they seem off the subject, so bear with them!

The last ten chapters explore different aspects of the love of God as it has been revealed in Scripture. They do so by setting God's love in the context of other truths about his divine life that he has revealed to us. These truths concern the doctrine of the Trinity and the attributes of God. Chapter 3 looks at how God's love is the first love because he is triune, and chapter 4 at how his love is perfectly ordered because he loves himself first. Chapter 5 contemplates the fact that God loves us as our Father and that he is ever-present with us (technically, his omnipresence). Chapter 6 considers the way in which God loves us without in any way needing us (his aseity), chapter 7 his sovereignty as lover, and chapter 8 the eternal and changeless (immutable) nature of his love. Chapter 9 scrutinizes the idea that God's love is without passion (his impassibility), asking why this idea matters and what it does and does not imply about how God loves us. Chapter 10 dwells on the perfect knowledge of God (his omniscience) and the ways in which it makes his love all the more wonderful. Chapter 11 describes how God's love always harmonizes with the requirements of his justice. Chapter 12 looks at the way God's love does not respond to but creates beauty in us.

Along the way I explore a number of important ways in which God's love is different from human love. As you study these differences, you should find that far from suggesting a deficiency in God's love, they are reasons why his love is immeasurably greater and more wonderful than our own. My argument is that our grasp of the unique manner of God's love deepens our grasp of its peerless magnitude: it is only when we see the similarities of God's love to human love and its differences from it that we see how great it is, how great he is.

This is a small book, and the love of God is a topic that would overflow even the weightiest tome, so please do not think that I will provide a comprehensive treatment of such a glorious subject. I am just going to scratch the surface. The approach is doctrinal, in that the argument largely proceeds by taking truths about God found in the Bible and using them to illuminate each other. Part of my aim is to show by example how spiritually and practically fruitful doctrinal theology can be, as C. S. Lewis testifies:

> For my own part, I tend to find the doctrinal books often more helpful in devotion than the devotional books, and I rather suspect that the same experience may await many others. I believe that many who find that 'nothing happens' when they sit down, or kneel down, to a book of devotion, would find that the heart sings unbidden while they are working their way through a tough bit of theology with a pipe in their teeth and a pencil in their hand.[5]

This is not intended as an academic work, which is why I have kept it largely free of academic apparatus and references to the literature on which it depends. If your appetite is whetted for the kind of theology you find here, then you will discover it richly and much better set out in the works of writers such as John Calvin, John Owen, Stephen Charnock, Francis Turretin and Herman Bavinck.

Lastly, I urge you not to rush past the meditations and the questions in them. We live in an age where we are deluged with information. Brian Appleyard is not alone when he comments that 'I feel that much of my life is ebbing away in the tide of minute-by-minute distraction'.[6] Wells speaks of how we suffer from 'a kind of cultural ADD'.[7] For the Christian the deluge can include Bible information. We may have woeful gaps in our Bible knowledge, but at the same time Christians in church cultures focused on expository preaching receive a lot of Bible teaching. Conscientious Christians might hear two passages preached on a Sunday, another passage at a midweek meeting and then might study seven more in their own

---

5. C. S. Lewis, 'On the Reading of Old Books', in Walter Hooper (ed.), *God in the Dock* (Grand Rapids: Eerdmans, 2014), p. 223.

6. Brian Appleyard, 'Distraction', *The Sunday Times*, 20 July 2008, http://bryanappleyard.com/distraction (accessed 4 Nov. 2014).

7. Wells, *Whirlwind*, p. 36, describing the argument of Maggie Jackson in her book *Distracted: The Erosion of Attention and the Coming Dark Age*.

daily readings. They may hear still more texts expounded if they listen online or download sermons and talks. That is a lot of Bible, and it can foster an unreflective approach to Scripture. No sooner have I listened to one passage expounded than my attention is called to another, and all the plates soon fall to the ground because there are too many spinning at once.

While I think it is a good idea for a church to read a lot of Scripture, including passages beyond the single text being preached, I think we would at the same time benefit from a church culture that encourages deeper meditation focused on fewer texts, creating the room for sustained reflection on the refreshing law of God. I have been grateful for those Christian meetings I have attended that have provided structured space for meditation on the way in which the truths of Scripture impact my life, leaving time for reflection and prayer. If you are going to read on in this book, I encourage you to do so with such time set apart. Even just a few minutes of silence will be better than nothing: the difference between no minutes and five is far greater than the difference between five and thirty. The meditations contain questions to guide your thinking.

Each chapter closes with a prayer intended to help you 'pray in' its teaching. The prayers are written in the first person not to encourage individualism, but because most people read on their own.

It is my prayer that this book will leave you with an expanded vision of the love of God, struck by both the uniqueness of its manner and the immeasurable greatness of its magnitude.

1. SMALL CREATURES WITH SIN-DARKENED MINDS

The difficulty for finite creatures in knowing God

It is amazing that we know anything at all about the love of God. Humanly speaking, it is highly unlikely that we would be able to know anything about God or to speak truthfully about him. Think first about the difference between created humans and the creator God. We are small, finite creatures. Even measured against the rest of the created universe we are inconceivably tiny. Astronomers estimate that there are hundreds of billions of galaxies in the universe. Our Milky Way is just one of them. They judge that within the Milky Way alone there are between 200 and 400 billion stars. Our sun is just one of them. But even the sun is vast compared to Earth: it would take more than a million planets like ours to fill the space of the sun. Earth is populated by 7 billion people, and you and I are just two of them. All but the most miniscule portion of the universe lies beyond our reach. How could we possibly think that we tiny creatures might know the mind of the God who created it? How could we speak truthfully of him? As God says to Job:

Where were you when I laid the foundation of the earth?
    Tell me, if you have understanding.
Who determined its measurements – surely you know!
    Or who stretched the line upon it?
On what were its bases sunk,
    or who laid its cornerstone,
when the morning stars sang together
    and all the sons of God shouted for joy?
(38:4–7)

Yet there is still more to God's unknowability than the fact that he made a vast universe that dwarfs us: he himself dwarfs us. God has something akin to physical immensity because he fills the entire creation:

Where shall I go from your Spirit?
    Or where shall I flee from your presence?
(Ps. 139:7)

Yet God does not fill the creation as the air fills a room. When my young son asks me if by clapping he is hitting God, the answer is that he is not. God is not some kind of pervasive physical particle; his immensity is the immensity of spirit. Not only that, but his immensity also transcends all size. It is not just that he is bigger than everything he has made, as if he were on the same scale as creation but higher up it. He is immeasurable not because he is so big but because he is beyond measurement itself.

God is beyond comparison with creation because he is the Creator, existing outside space and time in a way we cannot begin to imagine. His life and way of existing are different from ours and from everything else we know. All the things we are familiar with are made of matter, or, if they are like numbers or souls, are known to us through matter. There is nothing wrong with our being physical and embodied; it is as it should be, as God made it. When souls do exist apart from their bodies (after death and prior to the return of Christ), it is an anomaly that occurs only because of the presence of sin and death in the world. The natural created state of human beings is embodied, and so bodily knowing is our normal way of knowing. Yet God is not, in his divine nature, embodied. He is not spatial, but spirit (John 4:24). How then can we know him?

The Bible repeatedly testifies to the vital difference between humanity and God. Take Isaiah 40 for example. Isaiah comforts his people by proving that God is more than able to bring them home from their future exile in Babylon. God has said it, and it will happen, because his word stands for ever. He will come in might to gather up his lambs to bring them home. The obstacles to bringing the Israelites back are nothing for God. He is the creator God who needed no advice when he made the world. To him the nations are like a mere drop of water in a bucket, like mere specks of dust on weighing scales. All the beasts of Lebanon would not be enough as a sacrifice for him. The nations are nothing. God cannot be likened to any created thing:

> To whom then will you liken God,
>   or what likeness compare with him?
> (v. 18)

No motionless idol made by a craftsman can match him. God is the uncreated Creator who sits above the circle of the earth. To him we look like grasshoppers. Even our great rulers pass in an instant, like stubble blown in a storm. When Israel is faint and weary, she can look to the creator God who will give her strength, the God who renews young men and makes them soar like eagles. Isaiah teaches us that God is powerful and lifts up his people and triumphs over their enemies because he is different from them, because of the vast distance between God and everything else. He is the uncreated Creator, beyond all creatures. But here is the problem: we may rightly wonder, given God's transcendence, how we could ever even begin to know him, let alone speak to others about him and his love.

The difficulty for sinful creatures in knowing the holy God

The immeasurable greatness of God is not the only obstacle to our knowledge of him. A greater problem is the fact that as fallen creatures in a ruined world we are conceived in a state of spiritual

blindness. The entrance of sin into the world through the disobedience of our first parents Adam and Eve creates a twofold problem
for us. It spoils the revelation of God, and it ruins our spiritual sight,
so that we cannot see even what remains of that revelation in the
created world. What is more, even if we could see the revelation of
God in nature perfectly, that is not itself the revelation we need to
be saved from our fallen condition.

Ruined revelation

Consider first the way that the revelation of God itself has been
spoilt by sin. God walked in the garden and could be known by
Adam and Eve, but also the properly ordered natural world spoke
of God's glory to Adam. The first couple would have known God
by knowing themselves and each other, since they were themselves
the clearest image of God: 'Let us make man in our image, after our
likeness' (Gen. 1:26). The image of God would have been evident
in the unique features of humanity that fitted them for their task of
exercising dominion over the rest of creation as God's vice-regents.
The knowledge of God through the things he has created is what
theologians call 'natural' or 'general' revelation for Adam.

Even before sin entered the world, however, Adam also needed
'special' revelation from God, the spoken word that goes beyond
what nature says. Appearing to him in the garden, God gave verbal
instructions to Adam, setting before him the covenant in which he
should live and know God's blessing. He prescribed his work, his
rest and the single prohibition regarding the tree of the knowledge
of good and evil. When the first couple sinned and God came in
judgment, he announced the detailed curses for their disobedience.
Adam knew God both through the things he had made, especially
through himself and his wife, and through meeting him and hearing
him speak.

With the fall of Adam and Eve into sin, both these pathways
of revelation were disrupted. While nature still declares the glory of
God, it is now marred by sin. In its fallen state it is bound to decay
and groans as it waits for its future transformation (Rom. 8:18–25).
Humanity itself has been changed by the fall, and the image of God

in us has been ruined. The way we image God by ruling has been distorted. Instead of submitting to God as he ruled the creation for him, Adam submitted to Satan in the form of the serpent, a creature, and disobeyed God. The created order of God to man to creature was inverted to become creature to man to God. The created order of headship within marriage (1 Cor. 11:3) was inverted as Adam followed Eve's lead and pathetically failed to protect her from the serpent, and as strife then arose between them (Gen. 3:16). The capacities implied by being created in the image of God were also spoilt, so they no longer function properly.

That said, it is important to remember that we are still meaningfully in the image of God even after the fall. We read that Adam was created in the image of God and Seth in the image of Adam, implying that one born after the fall is still in God's image (Gen. 5:1–3). God tells Noah that whoever sheds the blood of a man will have his blood shed because 'God made man in his own image' (Gen. 9:6). And James rebukes his readers because they bless God while at the same time dishonouring those made in God's likeness by cursing them (Jas 3:9).

Nevertheless, we do not show God as clearly as we did. Most significantly, ready access to special revelation was closed to Adam and Eve when they were shut out from the garden of Eden and the way was blocked by the cherubim and the flaming sword (Gen. 3:24). Eden, like the tabernacle after it, was a dwelling place for God where he met with his people; exclusion from the garden meant exclusion from fellowship with God and the sound of his word.

This does not mean that the fallen creation leaves God wholly unknowable. Indeed, the opposite is true. The remaining revelation of God in the things he has made is plain for all to perceive. Even the fallen, groaning creation sings his praise so that we are surrounded by its voice (Ps. 19:1–6). Paul tells us that from the created things we know enough of God to render us guilty:

For the wrath of God is revealed from heaven against all ungodliness and unrighteousness of men, who by their unrighteousness suppress the truth. For what can be known about God is plain to them, because God has shown it to them. For his invisible attributes, namely, his eternal power and divine nature, have been clearly perceived, ever since the

creation of the world, in the things that have been made. So they are
without excuse. (Rom. 1:18–20)

There is a continuity here from the creation of the world down to
the present: throughout, God is known from creation. The general
revelation of God in nature even now makes every unbeliever
culpably ignorant. The rejection of natural revelation is more than
sufficient to condemn us. Yet the inversion of creation and the
corruption of the primary image bearer means that the revelation
is not as clear as it would have been in Eden.

What is more, the revelation of God available in the fallen natural
world is not a revelation that can bring us to new birth and open
our eyes to God. It is not a revelation of God's merciful plan to save.
We do see the goodness of God in his providential dealings with
the fallen world, as Paul explained to the people of Lystra:

> you should turn from these vain things to a living God, who made the heaven
> and the earth and the sea and all that is in them. In past generations he
> allowed all the nations to walk in their own ways. Yet he did not leave himself
> without witness, for he did good by giving you rains from heaven and fruitful
> seasons, satisfying your hearts with food and gladness. (Acts 14:15–17)

Nevertheless, the revelation of God in his providence is limited. It
shows his kindness, but it does not show his merciful plan to save
sinners. Even if we saw God's power as creator and his kindness as
sustainer clearly, we would not know his saving covenant. For fallen
man, even a return to the knowledge of God that Adam had in
creation would not suffice for salvation. A good case can be made
that Adam in the garden knew God as Father, Son and Holy Spirit,
but he did not know the Son as saviour; he did not need to know
him that way. Fallen people need a new revelation of God that goes
beyond the revelation of Eden: they need a revelation of the gospel.

Spiritual blindness

Consider, secondly, the loss of spiritual sight. After Adam we are
creatures with sin-darkened minds. Isaiah knew this. When he found

himself in the presence of God in the temple, he said, 'Woe is me! For I am lost; for I am a man of unclean lips, and I dwell in the midst of a people of unclean lips; for my eyes have seen the King, the LORD of hosts!' (Isa. 6:5). The apostle Peter had a similar reaction to the presence of Jesus when he saw the miraculous catch of fish: 'Depart from me, for I am a sinful man, O Lord' (Luke 5:8). Behind all later shying from the presence of God lies the primal instance of Adam in the garden of Eden: 'they heard the sound of the LORD God walking in the garden in the cool of the day, and the man and his wife hid themselves from the presence of the LORD God among the trees of the garden' (Gen. 3:8).

How can sinful God-fleeing creatures know God and speak truthfully about him? Left to ourselves, we cannot. We cannot by nature speak accurately about God. Since Adam fell we all turn from God, hiding from his presence, for we know that his holiness will destroy us. On our own, despite our pretensions to spirituality, the last thing we want to do is to know God. We are spiritually blind. Surrounded by the natural revelation of God but ever suppressing it, we are like a man on the dance floor of a nightclub amid the pulsating lights and pounding music, standing with his hands over his eyes and ears shouting, 'Not looking! Not listening!'

The impossibility of liberal theology

It is because of our spiritual blindness that the whole project of liberal theology is so deeply flawed, both in the technical sense of nineteenth-century liberal schools of thought and in the looser sense of any theology that sets aside God's Word in favour of human thoughts. In a liberal theology God becomes little more than a projection of the reigning culture's values. This means that his love ends up being remarkably like the love of whoever is in vogue at the moment, or at least was in vogue a few years ago (theologians take a while to catch up!).

Liberal theology is not, as it is often described even by its opponents, theology driven by reason. It is instead a form of culture Protestantism. It does not start with unaided reason and construct a theology on purely rational principles. The nearest anyone has come to that kind of approach would be René Déscartes in his *Meditations*, but it is not the project of liberal theology. Rather, liberal theology assumes the values of its own times. This was what horrified Karl Barth as the leading German liberal theologians signed up to support the Kaiser's war in 1914. This is what led J. Gresham Machen to conclude that liberal theology is in the final analysis 'pantheizing', since it identifies God with the world, or at least with the world in the particular form that the liberal theologian finds it.[1] As George Tyrell put it, the liberal historian stares down the well of history looking for the historical Jesus and sees his own face reflected in the bottom.[2] Considering the difficulty of knowing God warns us against such an approach to theology.

In sum, sin creates a twofold problem, objective and subjective. The objective problem is the ruin of the image in creation, and our exclusion from fellowship with the speaking God. The subjective problem – the problem in individuals – is our spiritual blindness. Given such obstacles, natural humanity cannot know God. Our only hope is to be found in a fresh and full objective revelation of God and a miraculous restoration of our spiritual sight. But how, given the obstacles, will God make such a revelation of himself? And how will he open blind eyes?

Meditation

Before turning to the Scriptures for answers to our questions, we pause to meditate on the humbling truths we have been exploring. We view the world through our own eyes. For much of the time this biological fact has the effect of limiting our horizons. We live unaware of the billions of other people on our planet and their activity. We do not see the far horizons of our own solar system, let

---

1. J. Gresham Machen, *Christianity and Liberalism* (Grand Rapids: Eerdmans, 2009), p. 55.

2. The image is a summary of Alfred Loisy's criticism of Adolf von Harnack. It can be found in George Tyrrell, *Christianity at the Cross-Roads* (London: Longmans, Green, 1910), p. 44.

alone our galaxy or universe. In our sinful nature we easily use this limitation of our sight to deceive ourselves into thinking that we occupy a more central place in the creation than we do. We loom large on a small stage. We are like the head boy at school who preens himself amid his acolytes, not realizing his true standing until he arrives at a university where nobody knows him.

Remembering the greatness of God, and how tiny we are as his creatures, humbles us. It makes us realize that God is far beyond us. He need have nothing to do with us unless he so chooses. A great distance separates us from him and makes it impossible for us to gain knowledge of him by ourselves.

- *Pause to reflect on the expanse of the created universe, and then on the transcendent greatness of its creator who sits above the circle of the earth.*

- *Meditate on the fact that you look like a grasshopper to God, and on the way in which he brings our greatest princes to nothing.*

We are further humbled by reflecting on the effects of the fall that range far and deep through the creation. There is no hope of knowing God in our fallen state. We enter the world as covenant breakers who constantly suppress the revelation of God. It is spiritually very important to remember what we are apart from the grace of God. This is particularly true of those privileged to be born within the boundaries of the covenant of grace who cannot remember living apart from the knowledge of God. The story of Adam is everyman's story, whether we remember it consciously or not.

- *Consider your natural spiritual blindness. Where would you be and what would your life be like if God had left you in the dark?*

In the light of our created finitude and sin-darkened minds we must renounce all attempts to fashion our own understanding of God. It is impossible for us to come to an accurate knowledge of God by ourselves. God is infinitely above us as creator. His image around us is not what it was, and it does not reveal his saving plan. His image in us is ruined. We are naturally blind to the revelation that remains, constantly suppressing it.

If we attempt to know God by ourselves, we will end up fashioning an idol, because we are naturally incapable of knowing him. We must be very alert to the danger of creating God in our own image. The apophatic (literally 'away from speech') instinct of ancient Christian mysticism can be taken too far. In an interesting turn of events it can even align itself with the postmodern suspicion of all truth claims to produce a theology radically sceptical of all theological statements (except its own!). This is clearly a wrong turn. Nonetheless, we would do well to learn from the ancient mystics the habit of identifying and setting aside our own idolatrous images of God.

We should do this specifically with our understanding of the love of God. What conceptions of God's love have we created from our own thoughts? Given the great difference between the holy creator God and sinful finite humanity, God's love is significantly unlike the common-currency definitions of love that we find in our human communities. Have we inferred from the statement 'God is love' that he is like *us* in his love? That is the way of liberal theology, but we cannot wag our fingers in judgment since it is a temptation we all face. We must all eschew our own ideas and inferences about what the love of God means or ought to mean for him. We must begin with renunciation, casting aside our idols, the images of God that stem from our own minds rather than from Scripture. This we do in repentance at the start of the Christian life, and we must go on doing it until we die and see God as he is with sinless sight.

- *What does the culture you live in tell you it means to be loving?*

- *Have you ever found yourself thinking or saying, 'God is love, so . . .'? What followed the 'so'? Where did it come from?*

- *If you were converted at an age you recall, what false images of God did you have to renounce in your conversion?*

- *What are the false ideas of God that most tempt you today? What would you most have him be that he is not?*

- *What convictions about God and creation will help you resist these temptations?*

Prayer

'Heavenly Father, I acknowledge how tiny I am as I measure myself against the things you have made. And then I think of you in your infinity and realize I cannot even begin to measure myself against you because you are beyond all scales and comparisons. You are the uncreated creator who exists beyond space and time in a way I cannot imagine. Your divine life is utterly unique. I am a grasshopper before you. The mightiest of men who look so permanent and strong to me for a while are nothing to you.

'I confess to you that I am not only small but also sinful. I acknowledge with shame the guilt of my sin-darkened mind. I know that I am by nature spiritually blind. I deserve to be left without the revelation of anything but your wrath.

'Show me where I have thought human thoughts about your love. Let me see where I have made an idol in the place of your true love. Forgive me for my pride in thinking I can know you by myself. Grant me deliverance from my idols. In Christ's name. Amen.'

2. GOD SPEAKS CREATURELY

In the first chapter I explained the twofold problem of fallen humanity: the revelation of God is ruined, and we are by nature spiritually blind. This twofold problem leaves us with a corresponding twofold need: we need the image of God restored so that he can be seen again, and we need to have our eyes opened to see him. More than that, we need the revelation of God expanded to include a revelation of his saving grace, because even the best natural revelation would not bring us the gospel that is God's answer to our fallen state. In short, we need a gospel to believe and the capacity to believe it.

The gift of the Son

Gloriously, this is what the Father in his mercy has given us. The Bible tells us that God is far above us, but also that he has drawn near. Herman Bavinck comments on how it presses both the transcendence and the closeness of God:

> There is certainly no book in the world which to the same extent and in the same way as the Holy Scripture supports the absolute transcendence

of God above each and every creature and at the same time supports
the intimate relationship between the creature and his Creator.[1]

God has come into intimate relationship with us supremely in the
person of his Son, the Lord Jesus Christ, and his Holy Spirit. Jesus
is the objective revelation of the Father.

As I explained in the last chapter, Scripture tells us not to make
images of God:

> To whom then will you liken God,
> > or what likeness compare with him?
>
> (Isa. 40:18)

Yet it also tells us that God himself has provided his own likeness:
Christ is 'the image of the invisible God' (Col. 1:15). Paul here uses
the Greek equivalent of the Hebrew word Isaiah uses for 'image'.
In effect, Isaiah 40:18 says that God must not be likened by us to
anyone, while Paul tells us that God gives us the image of himself
in Christ. The Lord is saying that we must not make God in the
likeness of man, but that he himself provides his own likeness in
the God-man Jesus Christ. The objective, saving revelation of God
is found in Christ.

Obviously God revealed himself prior to the incarnation of the
Son, but even then he did so through the Son. The Son was always
the agent of revelation. Jesus himself was perfectly clear that God
can be known only through him, the Son: 'no one knows the Father
except the Son and anyone to whom the Son chooses to reveal him'
(Matt. 11:27). This did not start being true when Jesus said it; it had
always been the case. It is a principle that is true at any point in human
history. The pattern of the Son's revealing the Father is always true
because it reflects the order of the persons of the Trinity: it is right
for the Father to be revealed by the Son who comes forth from him
in eternity. So if God was known in the Old Testament, as he surely
was, it was through the Son: the Son, even prior to his incarnation,

---

1. Herman Bavinck, *Our Reasonable Faith*, tr. Henry Zylstra (Grand
Rapids: Eerdmans, 1956), p. 132.

was the agent of revelation. For example, John tells us that Isaiah saw the glory of Jesus in the temple and spoke about him (John 12:41).

This is why Old Testament appearances of God are identified by most commentators in the history of the church as appearances of the Son. To use the technical terms, 'theophanies' (appearances of God) are commonly identified as 'Christophanies' (appearances of Christ). This does not mean that they were incarnations, since the incarnation was yet to come, but they were appearances. Indeed, the whole Old Testament is Christocentric. The promise of Christ was not something late in the Old Testament, let alone something extrinsic to it imposed by the New Testament. He was promised from right after the fall as the one struck by the serpent who would crush his head (Gen. 3:15). The Son is the one to whom all the types of the Old Testament point and in whom they are fulfilled. Paul is clear: 'all the promises of God find their Yes in him' (2 Cor. 1:20). We may rightly summarize all the objective, saving revelation of God as the revelation of the Son. The whole of the Bible points to him and finds its fulfilment in him.

But the revelation of God in the incarnation of the Son was new in its degree and in its fullness. In his hymn 'A Mighty Fortress' Martin Luther called Jesus Christ 'the Proper Man' (*der rechte Mann*), the one in whom God dwells fully and the one in whom his image is restored. In Jesus we see the perfect likeness of God. He is the 'radiance of the glory of God and the exact imprint of his nature' (Heb. 1:3).

Jesus is not just a new Adam; he is greater than Adam. Adam imaged God in his capacities and rule, but he was not God. Jesus images God by *being* God, the eternal Son of God incarnate as man. As Paul continues in Colossians, 'in him all the fullness of God was pleased to dwell' (1:19). Adam was like God, but Jesus is God. When we see Jesus, we see God's love. As Kevin Vanhoozer says, 'What we have in the incarnation is a God-given analogy, a fleshly representation, of the reality of the love of God.'[2]

---

2. Kevin J. Vanhoozer, 'Introduction: The Love of God – Its Place, Meaning, and Function in Systematic Theology', in Kevin J. Vanhoozer (ed.), *Nothing Greater, Nothing Better: Theological Essays on the Love of God* (Grand Rapids: Eerdmans, 2001), p. 25.

This should astound us. The Lord gave a revelation of himself in creation. We ruined it by sin. And what did God do? Did he leave us in the darkness of sin as we deserve? No. Did he just restore what was lost in Eden, putting us back into the covenant of life with Adam to attempt obedience again? No. Instead of abandoning us or taking us back to where we were, he responded to our sin by giving us his own Son. And in his Son we find a greater knowledge of God than Adam could ever have had, a knowledge of his mercy.

This is the Father's way: to bring an abundance of good out of our evil. He takes our sin and turns it to good. Think of Joseph at the end of Genesis. His brothers had intended selling him into slavery for evil, but God intended it to save Egypt and even the brothers themselves from famine (Gen. 50:20). God triumphed over their evil by bringing good out of it. Think of the cross of the Lord Jesus. As the murder of the Son of God it was the greatest evil ever perpetrated, and yet God had planned it from before the foundation of the world to accomplish the greatest good. God does not just turn the clock back. Instead of giving us Adam Mark 2, he achieves a new height of revelation by sending his Son as man: the God-man. God brings out of the darkness of sin a new, more perfect revelation of himself.

As the final revelation of God, Jesus is the ultimate prophet. Theologians have long spoken of the 'three offices' of Christ: he is our Prophet, our Priest and our King. Perhaps the most neglected of these three is the prophetic office. At least by implication we speak often of Jesus as our priest, sacrificing himself for our sins in his death on the cross. We speak often of him as our king, the risen Lord of our lives. Yet it is just as important for our salvation that he is the one in whom the Father is known, the prophet who reveals God to us: 'Whoever has seen me has seen the Father' (John 14:9). In Christ God has provided a more than sufficient revelation of himself that answers our greatest need.

The gift of the Holy Spirit

The generosity of the giving Father does not stop with the gift of his beloved Son. In fact, if salvation history had stopped at the incarnation, even at the death and resurrection of the Son, we could not be saved. We also need the Holy Spirit of God to dwell within us and to open our eyes to see the Son. To our dependence on Christmas and Easter we must add our dependence on Pentecost.

Apart from the Spirit's work in us, we could not see what has been done for us, and we could not become new creatures. Recall the parable of Lazarus and the rich man in Luke 16. The rich man in Hades pleads with Abraham to send Lazarus back from death to warn his brothers. Abraham answers, 'If they do not hear Moses and the Prophets, neither will they be convinced if someone should rise from the dead' (16:31). By nature we are so blinded by sin that, even if we were to see Jesus rise from the dead, and even if he came out of the tomb and stood nose to nose with us, we would still not recognize him as Lord. It is only the Holy Spirit who can open our eyes to see Jesus. As Paul beautifully puts it, 'we have received not the spirit of the world, but the Spirit who is from God, that we might understand the things freely given us by God' (1 Cor. 2:12).

In his infinite grace and mercy the Father gives us the Lord Jesus, and he gives us the Holy Spirit. By phrasing it like this I do not mean to suggest a division between the work of the Son and the work of the Spirit, as if we might ever actually have had one without the other. It was part of the work of the Son to die and to go to the Father in order to send us the Spirit: 'I tell you the truth: it is to your advantage that I go away, for if I do not go away, the Helper will not come to you. But if I go, I will send him to you' (John 16:7). Furthermore, all that Jesus himself did, he did by the power of the Spirit, even his death and resurrection. It was 'through the eternal Spirit' that he offered himself to God (Heb. 9:14), and he was declared Son of God 'according to the Spirit of holiness by his resurrection from the dead' (Rom. 1:4). In turn, the work of the Spirit is always about the Son: he is the Spirit of Christ (Rom. 8:9), and he glorifies Christ by taking what is his and making it known (John 16:14). It is in the inseparable co-working of the Son and the Spirit that we find both a new objective revelation of the Father and the subjective capacity to see it.

Created to communicate

In history the Father has revealed himself in the Son, and he opens
our eyes to see the Son by the work of his Spirit. He does this when
through the God-breathed words of the Bible he speaks to us in
power (2 Tim. 3:16; 1 Thess. 1:5). But how could the frail, creaturely
language of the Bible ever be enough to describe the revelation of
the creator God? How does God overcome the great gulf between
himself and his finite, sinful creatures? Can we understand more of
how the Spirit uses the words of ordinary human languages, both
the original languages and our translations, to describe the revelation
in the Son? In particular, how can God describe his love to us?

When we read about the love of God in Scripture, we are reading
words breathed out by God about himself. In Scripture God is
speaking about himself. To understand the nature of his love we
need first to consider exactly how it is that God speaks about himself.
What language does he speak to us? If I speak to you in French,
that makes a difference to how you understand me. What kind
of language does God use? How does he intend us to understand
his words?

One of the surprising things about the Bible is how very creaturely its language is, how it speaks using the raw vocabulary of
creation. God describes himself in tangible terms, using an astonishing range of images. There are some striking, even shocking,
comparisons: God is a lion (Isa. 31:4), an eagle (Deut. 32:11), a
fountain (Ps. 36:9), a sun and shield (Ps. 84:11), a fire (Heb. 12:29),
even a moth and dry rot (Hos. 5:12). Christ is a lion (Gen. 49:9), a
lamb (Isa. 53:7), even a hen (Matt. 23:37). How can God speak of
himself in such terms?

He can do so because he made the world as it is with the intention
of using it to reveal himself to us. The suitability of created things
for his purposes of revelation is not just a happy coincidence. God
did not make the world and then, when he decided to reveal himself,
find – ta-da! – that he could use the things in it to do so. Nor did
he settle on speaking of himself in creaturely terms as a second-best
alternative to some more direct way of communicating with us.
Theologians speak of God's condescending to speak to us. John
Calvin, for example, describes how God 'lisps' so that we can

understand him, like a nurse talking to a child.[3] It was always his
intention to speak to finite creatures, and he knew that to do so
he would need to speak in finite terms we could grasp. We should
not, therefore, think that there is something wrong or unfortunate
with God's speaking in this way. He fully intended this way
of communicating as his first-choice method. He designed the
creation to be used like this from the outset. Isaiah tells us that God
knows and plans the end from the beginning (Isa. 46:9–11), and
this applies as much to his plans for revelation as it does to
everything else.

In God's mind, because he is supremely purposeful, the end
precedes the beginning. He designs the beginning to serve the
purpose of the end. This means that the creation was fashioned for
the purposes of redemption and revelation. While we rightly wonder
how created things could ever be used to describe the uncreated
God, this is the very reason for which God made them. God did
not make the world, watch it fall and then come up with Plan B, the
plan of redemption and revelation. The revelation of God in Christ
was the goal of creation, not an accidental by-product when the
world went wrong. Jesus Christ was the lamb slain before the foundation of the world (1 Peter 1:19–20; Rev. 13:8). God planned his
death (Acts 2:23) and chose his people (Eph. 1:4) even before the
universe began.

As God predestined his Son, so he planned the Bible as the
revelation of his Son for the church. Every jot and tittle of Scripture
was eternally purposed by the Holy Spirit. All of the ways in which
the Bible uses created things to describe the revelation of the Father
in the Son were planned. The things used in the Bible to describe
God were created in order to do just that. This is why the created
ordinances of marriage and the Sabbath can be taken up in the order
of redemption and applied to the work of Christ. Christ is the bridegroom for the church (Eph. 5:23), and he provides our rest (Heb.
4:1–10): this is no divine afterthought.

---

3. John Calvin, *Institutes of the Christian Religion*, ed. John T. McNeill,
tr. Ford Lewis Battles, 2 vols., Library of Christian Classics 20–21
(Philadelphia: Westminster, 1960), 1.13.1, 1.121.

God uses the creation to describe himself to humans. The panoply of created things serves the relationship between God and us. Humanity is, therefore, the pinnacle of God's creation, and the rest of creation is there to be used as the medium of his communication with us. This is a remarkable thought. Some non-Christian world views claim the title 'humanistic', but we see here why Christianity has been described as the true humanism, since it gives an extraordinarily exalted position to humanity, insisting that a human is far more than an animal, far more than a 'naked ape'. The whole world is designed to be a field of communication between God and humanity.

When you next go to a safari park or zoo and see a lion, ask yourself, Why the lion? The answer must be this: God created his world as he did in order to make himself known to humanity within it, so the chief reason he made the lion was so that he could use it to describe himself. Of course the lion has other purposes: it is to hunt antelope and to feature in documentaries. But its greatest office, its highest honour, is to be used to describe God and Christ. Or consider the stars. At the heart of their purpose is their role in illustrating to Abraham and all his descendants the extent of the nation of believers that would be his children (Gen. 15:5). The vastness of the heavens serves to illustrate the extent of the kingdom of God.

God speaks analogically

Even if we understand that the use of created things to reveal himself was part of God's plan, we may yet wonder how they can do so. How can mere created things image the invisible God? How can he use them to describe his love? They can do so because they reflect, in a small way, his perfections. When God made the world, he pronounced it 'good' and 'very good' (Gen. 1:10, 12, 18, 21, 25, 31). All real things are in some way good, since God is the only creator and all things are made through his word: 'without him was not any thing made that was made' (John 1:3). The devil cannot create; he can attempt only to ruin what God has made. God himself is the highest good, the sum of all goodness. As the Lord Jesus

himself states, 'No one is good except God alone' (Mark 10:18). All
true goodness is found in God. If, therefore, created things have
some good in them, then that good is a reflection of the God who
possesses all goodness without limit.

It is the existence of goodness in creatures that enables them to
reveal God truly. Divine perfections are imaged in the goodness of
created things. We can use the same words of God and of created
things because God is the cause of all created things and has made
their goodness after his own likeness. If, for example, we say that a
woman is 'righteous' and God is 'righteous', we can use the same
word of both because the woman has her righteousness from God
as her cause, in whom it first exists perfectly. We might express the
same idea more simply: when the creator God makes things, he
leaves his fingerprints all over them in the form of reflections of
his goodness, so we can describe him by speaking about the things
he has made that contain those traces. Stephen Charnock uses a
similar illustration:

> Hath not everything some stamp of God's own being upon it, since
> he eminently contains in himself the perfections of all his works?
> Whatsoever hath being, hath a footstep of God upon it, who is all being;
> everything in the earth is his footstool, having a mark of his foot upon
> it; all declare the being of God, because they had their being from God.[4]

This does not mean that the differences between the creation and
God are erased. While created things image the perfections of God,
they do not do so by being the same as him. The Creator–creature
distinction always remains in place. Even when the Creator and the
creature come closest together in the incarnation of God in Christ,
the two natures remain distinct. They are perfectly united, but they
are not mixed together. God reveals himself in the things he has
made; he does not turn himself into them.

Apart from the Lord Jesus Christ in whom the fullness of God
was pleased to dwell, all other created things can image God only

---

4. Stephen Charnock, *The Existence and Attributes of God* (Grand Rapids:
Baker, 1996; repr. 2000), 1.388.

partially. A rock, for example, images the dependability of God, but it does not image the fact that he is alive. A lion images his strength, but it does not image his wisdom. Fire images the way he consumes sin, but it does not image that he does so rationally and in a controlled way. Created things are both like God and different from him. In the ways they reflect his perfections they are like him, but in their finitude they are unlike him.

This combination of similarity and difference shows that when God describes himself using the things he has made, he speaks analogically. We use an analogy when we describe one thing in terms of another that it is like in certain respects but different from in others. For example, Scripture uses an analogy when it speaks of the church as a body. The church is like a body in certain respects: it has different parts that work together while doing different things. But the church differs from a body in important ways: it is not made of flesh and it does not have hair or cut its fingernails. The analogy involves likeness, but not complete identification. This is why biblical revelation is correctly termed 'analogical'.

Created things can, with God's own authority in his Word, be used to describe him, but they cannot be entirely identified with him. Moreover, the very richness and diversity of the Bible's description of God shows us that we must read it analogically. God cannot simultaneously be a rock in every way that a rock is a rock, and fire in every way that fire is fire, and water in every way that water is water. For these biblical descriptions to be coherent, they must be read analogically, taking some aspects of one and some aspects of the other to be true of God.

The self-reflecting God reflects himself

The idea that God creates images of himself makes sense given who he is. God's own existence is an existence in which he eternally reflects himself. The Son reflects the Father: he is 'the radiance of the glory of God and the exact imprint of his nature' (Heb. 1:3). The possibility of God's reflecting himself in another is established by the way in which the being of the Father is eternally reflected in his Son. God eternally communicates himself to himself, Father to Son, the one

God to the one God. Were God a monad (as Muslims believe Allah is), we might well wonder how he could image himself in the world since he would not *be* the self-imaging God. But since within himself he is eternally self-imaging, his self-imaging in created things is an appropriate outpouring of his own eternal relations.

The Son is the image of the Father. This is why it was fitting for him to be the one who came as a man to reveal the Father. Because of who he is in eternity, he becomes who he is in time. The eternal radiance of God's glory becomes the one who reveals his glory in history, who says as he approaches his death, 'glorify your Son that the Son may glorify you' (John 17:1). It was when God became man that the Holy Spirit was most able to describe God by using human language. In the incarnation God the Son himself has his own human nature, making him eligible for the most creaturely and human descriptions. Now he has soul and flesh and blood. Now he has hunger and tears. And now he has death itself. Hence we read that Jesus 'grew and became strong' (Luke 2:40), that he was tempted and hungered (Luke 4:2), thirsted (John 19:28), grew tired (John 4:6), wept (John 11: 35) and died (John 19:30).

The self-interpreting revelation of divine love

How does this point about analogy help us understand the way in which God speaks about his love? If we were to lose the Bible and be left with only the statement 'God is love', we might conclude that God is exactly like us when he loves. There would be no other passages to warn us that God is different from us or to compel us to refine our view of his love. We would not then know that revelation is analogical, and we might think that God's love is identical with our own. We do not, however, have the statement in isolation. We have it in the same Bible that warns us about comparing created things to God, and that stresses how far above the creation God is. And we have it in the context of the whole Bible, which contains a range of descriptions of God that show us how different he is from us in many respects.

How then do we work out the ways in which God's love is like the love we know in creation, and in what ways is it different? It is easy to grasp that the statement 'God is a rock' does not mean that he is made of stone. What are the conclusions we should not draw from the fact that God is love? We come to understand the similarities and differences by reading together the different biblical descriptions of God and allowing them to regulate one another. When we soak ourselves in the Bible and ponder its message and coherence, we find it interprets itself. It is not our interpretation that matters. It is neither your ideas nor my ideas that are determinative. It is not the ideas of a presbytery, a bishop or a pope that tell us what the Bible means. It is the Bible's interpretation of itself that counts. The great Protestant principle is that the Bible regulates its own meaning, as one passage sheds light on another. The self-existent God is self-interpreting: just as God exists from himself and no other, so his word interprets itself to us and submits to no other.

The Bible must be read as a whole because God is simple

There is a deep theological reason that explains why divine revelation must be read together as a whole like this. If God were made up of lots of different, separable parts, then we might safely be able to read one statement about him without reference to any others. He would be like a cargo ship that carries hundreds of containers from different places, which will go their separate ways on arrival. The contents of each container could safely be described without reference to any other container. God is not like that, because he is simple.

The simplicity of God means that he is not made up of parts that could be separated. There are no distinct components of his being. His divine life is not a complex composition of different elements. Even his attributes are not different parts of his being. God could not lose any of his life and still be God. Whereas I might lose a limb or my sight and still be me, God has no dispensable parts. He could not lose his love or his holiness or his sovereignty and still be God. While you can distinguish and even divide my human life into its diverse parts, for example into body and soul, God is not diverse in that way: 'I AM WHO I AM' (Exod. 3:14). No one has ever put God together, and no one can take him apart. All that God is, is God.

Given divine simplicity, it is imperative that we integrate all of the different elements of biblical revelation with one another. Simplicity prohibits us from isolating the attribute of divine love from God's other attributes. Indeed, we cannot rightly understand any one of God's attributes apart from the rest. The attempt to read God's love in the light of other aspects of his divine life is not only necessary because Scripture speaks about God analogically in statements that together fill out the picture of who he is. It is also necessary because of God's own attribute of simplicity. Given who God is, we must integrate our understanding of his different attributes because he is himself one and simple.

It is worth noting too that the simplicity of God keeps a study of divine love in a proper perspective because it prevents us thinking that we are studying an aspect of his life that is more important than any other. Simplicity means that none of his attributes is prior to any other. We cannot say that God is more one aspect of his life than he is another. He is not more just than he is loving, or more loving that he is just. John says both that 'God is love' and that 'God is light' (1 John 1:5). God is all of his attributes all of the time.

Proper and improper differences

In the following chapters I will consider especially the ways in which God's love and human love differ. The differences will be of two sorts. With the first sort we will find that our own human love does not and should not reflect God's love. These will be points of proper difference. Human love is appropriately different from God's love, because it is human and not divine. It would be wrong to seek to conform our love to God's love at these points, since it is meant to be different. In some cases it is impossible for us to be like God because his attributes are incommunicable: they cannot be shared with others. For example, God's love is timeless, because he is eternal. We will never be eternal in the way God is, so our love is rightly different at that point. Such differences make the comparison of human with divine love an analogy rather than a strict univocal, point-for-point identification.

With the second sort of difference we will find that human love does, and should, reflect divine love, because God has communicable attributes in which we can share. Differences remain because our love reflects God's love imperfectly. Human love falls short of what it ought to be because of sin. In a perfect world these differences would not be because they arise when our love is morally flawed in some way. We should, therefore, seek to conform our love more closely to God's love at these points, since it is meant to be the same. Of course, even morally perfect human love would still be smaller than God's love, and in that sense could only ever be analogous to it and never identical with it.

With both types of difference we will be led to marvel at God's love, either because his love is so different from ours in kind, or because it is the perfect form of the love with which we ourselves so weakly love.

Meditation

We must pause to rejoice in the simple fact that God has made himself known. Despite our sin, and the darkness into which it has plunged us, God has not cast us off. When we broke one covenant in Adam, God initiated another, founded in his Son and sealed by his Spirit. His amazing grace ought always to surprise us. May it continue to thrill us even if we have walked with the Lord for many years.

- *How are you tempted to take the saving grace of God for granted?*

- *Consider what you deserve from God, and what riches he has given you in his Son and Spirit.*

It is a wonderful mercy to have Jesus as our sacrificing priest and protecting king, but it is also a wonderful mercy to have him as our revealing prophet, making the love of God known to us. We should consciously recall and give thanks for Jesus the prophet of God's love. We honour him as our prophet by relying on him alone for the revelation of God. We dishonour him when we look elsewhere for the mind of God.

- *How much consideration have you given to the prophetic office of Christ as revealer?*

- *How might you make a habit of dwelling with gratitude on this aspect of the work of Christ?*

Christmas would have no effect were it not for Pentecost. The work of the Son is revealed to us by the work of his Spirit. So often contemporary thinking about the Spirit is preoccupied by debates about his gifts, but only a handful of biblical texts discuss those phenomena. Many more concern the Spirit's wider work in creation, in Israel, in the birth, life, death and resurrection of the Son, and in authoring the Scriptures. In our own lives it is only by the regenerating and illuminating work of the Spirit that our eyes are opened to see clearly the revelation of God in the Son. Father, Son and Holy Spirit: all the works of the Trinity are undivided. How much we depend on him!

- *When you think of the 'work of the Holy Spirit', which aspects of his work do you focus on?*

- *Which elements of the broad biblical picture might merit more reflection?*

The Bible contains an amazing panoply of images for the simple God. Each of these was planned by God himself before he created the world. He made the things he made so that he could use them to describe himself to us in the Bible. Think of the rich, thick layers of description we find in the sixty-six books authored by the Spirit over fifteen hundred years. Marvel at the genius and skill of the divine author who placed together so many intricately drawn tiles into such a rich mosaic, all so that he could make himself known to tiny, helpless creatures with sin-darkened minds.

- *List some of the biblical images for God. Reflect on what each one contributes to our understanding of who he is and how he loves.*

Prayer

'Heavenly Father, I confess that I am small and sinful in your eyes, yet you have given your Son as prophet to make yourself known to me. In seeing him, I have seen you.

'You have given your Spirit to breathe the Scriptures and to open my eyes. In them you speak to me in terms I can understand. What are humans that you have made creation to speak to them? Yet you designed the world to be used to speak about yourself.

'I ask that you would forgive me for the ways in which I have fashioned you in my own image.

'Help me to listen to your word and not to my own head, to rejoice that you have made yourself known, and to delight to hear you speak through your Son and your Spirit. Fix my eyes and thoughts on Jesus. In his name. Amen.'

3. LOVE BEFORE ALL OTHER LOVES

We have seen that God is infinitely different from us as creator and as holy, and yet he reveals himself to us in his Son, describes him in creaturely language in the Bible and opens our eyes to understand it by his Spirit. The triune God, Father, Son and Holy Spirit, gives us knowledge of himself as an unmerited gift. As we turn to consider the love of God we must reckon with both the difference of God from man and his revelation in creaturely, even human, likenesses.

How should our thinking about God's love be affected by the fact that he is so different from us? How is his love alike and unlike created loves? How is our grasp of God's love affected by the analogical manner of his revelation? Recall some of the questions I posed about the love of God in introducing this book: When we say 'God is love', does God's love come and go? Might he fall in and out of love? Is his love an act of will and resolve, or a feeling? Does God have emotions as we do? Each of these questions raises the underlying issue: How is God like us?

We have the essence of an answer already: God is different from us, and yet we are sufficiently like him that he can be described in the Bible using creaturely analogies. He is so vastly different from us that we must be extremely careful not to fashion him in our likeness, but he has himself provided his own likeness for us in his Son. In describing the Son, he has spoken to us in a language we can understand, but he has spoken carefully, using one description to regulate the implications of another. When God says he is love, we must ask how the other things he says about himself inform our understanding of that love. In other words, we discover the full meaning of the statement 'God is love' when we read it alongside the other descriptions of God in the Bible. In a sense this whole book – indeed all theology – is just a reading lesson, a study in how to read God's speech about himself.

It is to that process of reading that we now turn. In this and the following chapters I will attempt to apply the understanding set out so far to the love of God, exploring several ways in which the love of God is made known to us in Christ, and yet is made known as different from, and marvellously greater than, our own love. In this chapter we will explore one of the first types of difference between divine and human love, one that should exist and always will exist. It is a difference that will bring us to marvel at the uniqueness of God's love.

Defining love

'In the beginning, God' (Gen. 1:1). God is before all his creatures. His love, therefore, is different from our love because it is the first love of all, the original and ultimate love, the love anterior to all other loves. His love is the first love that ever existed and is, therefore, the love that provides the definition and test for all other loves. There was no definition of love that existed before his love, into which his love then fitted as the first actual instance of love. There was no already existing definition of love prior to God's love, because there was nothing prior to God. God and his love precede all definitions. More than that: God constitutes all definitions. It is God's love that defines love, not any abstracted definition, let alone our human love. God does not just love before anyone else in the way that one singer sings a Schubert *Lied* before another. He is like Schubert himself, the one who wrote the song. God *is* love. Apart from God there is no definition of love.

Triune love

How is God love in himself? In particular, given that there is only one God, how could he love before he created any other being to love? The Bible reveals that God is love because in the life of the one God there is distinction, the distinction between the three persons of the Trinity: the Father, the Son and the Holy Spirit. These distinctions do not imply that there are three gods. Rather, the three persons exist in the one being of God without dividing God in three. The Bible says that 'The Lord our God, the Lord is one' (Deut. 6:4), *and* it says that Jesus is the 'one Lord' (1 Cor. 8:6), *and* that 'the Lord is the Spirit' (2 Cor. 3:17). Love, therefore, exists in the life of God as the three persons of the Trinity love one another, before they create anything outside themselves.

We read in John 3:35, 'the Father loves the Son'. At the baptism of Jesus and later at his transfiguration the Father declares from heaven, 'This is my beloved Son' (Matt. 3:17; 17:5). Likewise, the Son loves the Father. This is evident supremely in his death: as his hour approaches Jesus says, 'I do as the Father has commanded me, so that the world may know that I love the Father' (John 14:31). The Father sends the Son he loves, and the Son comes in loving obedience. This is the intra-trinitarian love of God, the love of the Father for his only-begotten Son and the love of the Son for his Father. Love exists eternally in God only because there is differentiation within God between the equally divine persons. The Father and the Son are one God, but the Father is not the Son, and the Son is not the Father. It is this trinitarian love that is the first love, an eternal love that stands before all other loves. This is the love that defines all other loves.

It is instructive to note at this point the contrast with the Islamic understanding of Allah. We read in the Qur'an, 'Say: "He is God, One, God, the Everlasting Refuge, who has not begotten, and has not been begotten, and equal to Him is not any one."[1] The Qur'an rejects the doctrine of the Trinity by denying that there is any begetting within the being of Allah, although when it describes the doctrine of the Trinity that it rejects, it is a strange description:

> And when God said, 'O Jesus son of Mary, didst thou say unto men, "Take me and my mother as gods, apart from God"?' He said: 'To Thee be glory! It is not mine to say what I have no right to. If I indeed said it, Thou knowest it, knowing what is within my soul, and I know not what is within Thy soul; Thou knowest the things unseen. I only said to them what Thou didst command me: "Serve God, my Lord and your Lord."'[2]

There are two misunderstandings of the doctrine of the Trinity evident here. The Qur'an seems to hold that the Trinity consists of the Father, Jesus and Mary. Had Muhammad met idolatrous Christians who seemed to worship Mary? Perhaps that explains his mistaken description of the doctrine. The Qur'an also maintains that a trinitarian conception of God implies that there are three gods: the Father and two gods beside him. This is the very teaching the Bible and the church deny.

That aside, while Muslims believe Allah is loving if he forgives sin, their denial of the Trinity means they cannot believe he is eternally love. They affirm a monadic doctrine of God, one that allows no differentiation within his life, so that Allah is eternally alone. Someone who is eternally alone cannot be love. Considered apart from creation, Allah has no object of love, and is not himself love. Only the God of the Bible can have the eternal ground and definition of love within himself.

Always love

Here is an aspect of God's perfection: that he is always loving in his

---

1. *The Koran: Interpreted*, tr. Arthur J. Arberry (Oxford: Oxford University Press, 1983; repr. 2008), Sura 112, p. 667.
2. Ibid., Sura 5, p. 119.

own inner life. The Father eternally delights in his Son and his Spirit, the Son in his Father and Spirit, the Spirit in the Father and Son. This is who he always is. The trinitarian relations are untroubled, undisturbed, eternally constant and full, overflowing with love and delight.

Even as the Son died under the curse of sin, the relationship of the same Son *as God* to his Father remained intact: the eternal Son bore the curse on sin in his human nature. Because the sin he atoned for was human sin committed by men, he could bear it effectively only if he bore it in his human nature. This is the reasoning of the writer to the Hebrews, who argues that Christ 'had to be made like his brothers in every respect, so that he might become a merciful and faithful high priest in the service of God, to make propitiation for the sins of the people' (2:17). The Son of God died as man, bearing the punishment for sin, while in his own divine nature he remained in perfect loving union with the Father. It is important to note that these distinctions do not divide the person of Christ: the human nature in which he dies is *his* nature, the nature of *one and the same* divine Son. The natures are distinguished, but not separated.

The idea of the Trinity being ruptured in the atonement preaches well because it sounds so dramatic, but it plays havoc with the doctrine of God and the doctrine of the atonement itself. It would amount to a denial of the doctrine of the Trinity, because if God might remain God while the triune relations were shattered, then they would not be a necessary part of who he is. If he could be non-trinitarian and still be God, then the Trinity would not be part of his identity; it would be a dispensable add-on to his being. The idea of the Son's being separated from the Father as God would also fail to satisfy the just requirements for atonement, since the substitute who suffered as God would not be identical in nature with the humans who deserved to suffer. Even in the midst of the horror of the cross, the Father and the Son remained united in love as God.

God is always love. Love is not something he opts to be from a list of choices each day. 'Hmm, whom shall I be today? Shall I be good, evil, loving, unloving?' Many people in our own times create and recreate their own social identities from day to day. Think of the way in which Madonna or Lady Gaga have periodically (perhaps that underestimates the frequency!) reinvented themselves. But God is not Proteus. He is no shape-shifter. He is who he is, always. He is perfect love, for ever. There is to God's inner relations a completeness, and it is the completeness of love. The Holy Trinity is the eternal fullness of love.

The order of being and the order of knowing

Here then is a marked difference between human and divine love. Divine love, God's love, triune love, comes first. It, not human love, is the definition of love. It is not to be defined by other loves, such as marital love. It defines all other loves. This is important for understanding how the analogies used in the Bible work. The Bible does not depict God's relationship to his people as a marriage because God's love is like human marital love. It is the other way round: the Bible depicts God's love as a human marriage because human love is a reflection of God's love. God's love comes first and provides the definition.

This is not always how we come to know God's love in our own lives. If you grew up as a non-Christian and were converted later in life, then you already had all sorts of definitions of love in your mind when you first heard that God is love. Perhaps you knew the love of a father and mother, brothers and sisters, friends, a husband or wife. Then you heard the gospel, and the gospel depicted God as a loving father and a bridegroom coming in search of his bride, laying down his life for his friends. You understood human love first, and then you heard it used as an analogy for divine love. In the order of knowing that you experienced, human love came first. But in the order of being, the order of reality, God's love came first. He existed before you were born, before the world was made. He defined love before all other loves. You probably came to understand human love and then divine love, but divine love still came first.

If this was your experience, then you will have found that the concept of love you brought with you when you came to Christ has been progressively corrected and refined by the Scriptures. You have seen how some of its aspects are inappropriate if applied to God. If this is so, then you have experienced in your Christian life what

I am trying to do in this book: Scripture has interpreted itself to you as one analogy has regulated another.

On the other hand, if you were raised within the covenant people of God, then your order of knowing may have been closer to the order of being. When someone in her testimony says that she cannot recall a day when she did not know the love of Jesus, she is saying that her memory of God's love goes as far back as her memory of her family's love. This is how David described his own experience:

> Yet you are he who took me from the womb;
>> you made me trust you at my mother's breasts.
> On you was I cast from my birth,
>> and from my mother's womb you have been my God.
> (Ps. 22:9–10)

David here echoes the language of God's foundational promise to Abraham 'to be God to you and to your offspring after you' and to 'be their God' (Gen. 17:7, 8). David is saying that he had faith in God from the womb, a fact explicable only by the miraculous work of the Holy Spirit, such as he worked later in John the Baptist who was indwelt by the Spirit before birth and 'leaped in her womb' when Mary greeted Elizabeth (Luke 1:15, 41). An infant's faith cannot be the same as adult faith since it lacks the full cognitive element that comes with mental understanding, but it is nonetheless described as faith in this psalm. Reformed writers have spoken of it as seminal (as in 'seed') or radical (as in 'root') faith.[3] A person who grew up with such faith may have less of a wrong understanding of love to unlearn than someone who has lived long outside Christ. Even so, all Christians' understanding of love will always need to be redrawn again and again until we see God as he is on the new earth.

---

3. For the idea of a seed of faith in infants, see John Calvin, *Institutes of the Christian Religion*, ed. John T. McNeill, tr. Ford Lewis Battles, 2 vols., Library of Christian Classics 20–21 (Philadelphia: Westminster, 1960), 4.16.20. For the language of both seed and root, see Francis Turretin, *Institutes of Elenctic Theology*, ed. James T. Dennison, tr. George Musgrave Giger, 3 vols. (Phillipsburg: P. & R., 1992–7), 15.14.13.

Meditation

What difference does the fact that God's love is the first love make to us? We prize love. Even in its fallen human forms we seek it, we long for it, we esteem it. You need only to look at the constant outpouring of love songs in the pop music charts to see how preoccupied we are by love: hits when I was writing this book included 'Bad Romance', 'Te Amo' and 'Your Love Is My Drug'. The television channels are full of programmes that make a spectacle of human love, from an old British show like *Blind Date* through to the more recent American *Bachelorette*. Endless dating websites display lists of 'Singles in your area', inviting us to look for love.

And it is not just the non-Christian world that is on a quest for the perfect relationship. The Christian publishing market is flooded with books written to help Christian singles move towards marriage, and to help married couples improve their marriages. Many of these books are helpful and I do not mean to criticize them. Nevertheless, we will never find love among ourselves in flawless form, and much of the searching is hopelessly idealistic. Young people with a dreamy conception of human marriage as a perpetually tranquil idyll are setting themselves up for disappointment. There is no such thing as an always harmonious, constantly delightful human relationship in this life.[4] Search for it, and you will meet only disappointment. But there is one such love. In one place, in the eternal life of the triune God, flawless love flourishes. We should stand silenced before the perfect love of God, and should adore him for it, for who he is in his triune life.

- *How have you idealized human relationships? In what ways have you been disappointed by them?*

- *Think through the life of Jesus to find ways in which the persons of the Trinity reveal their love for each other.*

---

4. When my wife proofread this page, she remonstrated with me that ours is such a marriage, thus ironically proving the point!

We rightly adore God for what he has done, for his benefits freely given to us in creation and supremely in redemption. We adore him for giving us his Son and for the salvation won for us on the cross. But we should not think that the cross is an addition to the love of God. It does not make God more love after it than he was before it. God does not need the cross to be who he is, as if he lacked something without it. Rather, the cross is an expression of who God already was prior to it. The Father sends the Son because he already loves us, and his love for us is an expression of the love that exists eternally in the Trinity. The incarnation is the embodiment of who God already is. God's acts in history themselves show us that, prior to them, he is love. God's being of love precedes his works of love. We should meditate, therefore, both on what he has done for us and on what it reveals of who he is in himself, and always this way round, as Herman Bavinck explains: 'The truth which at first we love especially because it gave us life, thereupon becomes more and more dear to us because of itself, because of what it reveals to us concerning the Eternal Being.'[5]

We do not have access to the being of God by some other means, apart from his works. We cannot, against what some Christian mystics have thought, ascend into the darkness at the top of Mount Sinai to immerse ourselves in the essence of God, leaving behind his deeds and our knowledge of them through creaturely language. That is to seek a way of knowing God that he has not provided, and it is to imply some kind of deficiency in his chosen means of revelation. There is no such deficiency: it is the honour of created things to be used as the vehicles of God's self-revelation in the Bible, an honour that cannot be taken from them in favour of another means of knowing. We know the being of God through his works, and we delight in both what God has done and, through that, in who he is.

- *Reflect on the connection between what God has done and who he is.*

- *Have you sometimes detached gratitude for God's benefits from adoration of his being?*

---

5. Herman Bavinck, *Our Reasonable Faith*, tr. Henry Zylstra (Grand Rapids: Eerdmans, 1956), p. 130.

Prayer

'Triune God, Father, Son and Holy Spirit, may I learn who you are from what you have revealed of your eternal relations of love. Your triune love is eternal. It precedes all other loves. It fits no definition of love because it forms the definition of love. It is untroubled, undisturbed and eternally constant. You will not one day decide not to be love, because this is who you are. Your triune love is a flawless, flourishing love. I praise you, triune God of love, for the prior perfection of your divine life.

'God and Father of the Lord Jesus Christ, I praise you that you revealed your love for your Son when you said, "This is my beloved Son, with whom I am well pleased; listen to him." Help me to listen to him because he is the one you love.

'Eternal Son of God, I praise you for your love for the Father shown in your perfect obedience to him, even unto death. You have said that I must learn from your obedience that you love the Father. Teach me this.

'Holy Spirit of God, I praise you that you are the bond of love between the Father and the Son, that the Son offered himself to the Father and was raised through you. I praise you that through the Word you breathed I have come to know the Son, and through him the Father.

'Lord God, help me not to measure your love by human love, but always to remember that your love is different from human love because it is the first love of all. Forgive me for the times when I have forgotten that and have tried to squash you into human boxes. Thank you that your acts reveal your being of love. Help me to prize you for who you are. In Christ's name. Amen.'

4. LOVE IN PERFECT PROPORTION

The story of Abelard and Heloise

The priority of God's love as the first love discussed in the previous chapter is an example of a difference between divine and human love that ought to exist and always will exist. If we try to make our human love the defining love, then we are seeking to oust God from his proper place. In this chapter we turn to a difference between divine and human love that arises because of sin, a difference that ought not to be, and a difference that will not be in the new creation. To bring it into sharp relief I begin by telling part of the story of the medieval lovers Abelard and Heloise. This is a story that brings out the disordered character of human loves. It is also one of the most tragic love stories ever told in truth or fiction.

Abelard was a phenomenon in the French church of the twelfth century. At a young age he became Master of the Schools of Paris where he taught philosophy and theology to crowds of enraptured students. He was proud of his achievements, and it was his pride that led him to temptation, as he explains in an autobiographical piece: 'I thought I was the only philosopher in the world and had nothing to fear from anyone, and now I began to give free reign to my lust.'[1]

His lust came to rest upon the young Heloise. She was beautiful, but it was her extraordinary learning and culture that attracted his attention. Pre-eminent among women, he thought her a conquest suited to his own brilliance. Abelard's self-confidence extended to his seductive powers: 'I was famous myself at the time, young, and exceptionally good-looking, and could not imagine that any woman I thought worthy of my love would turn me down.'[2] But even he was surprised by the ease with which he gained access to Heloise. Her uncle Fulbert was ambitious, so he gave Abelard full charge of her education, even allowing him to administer corporal punishment. Abelard later commented, 'The simplicity of the man just staggered me, as if he had set a ravening wolf to watch over a lamb.'[3]

Abelard and Heloise studied together, but soon, as he put it, 'we exchanged more words of love than of lessons, more kisses than concepts'.[4] They abandoned all restraint. Up to that point, as Étienne Gilson strikingly puts it, this 'is no love story, but the tale of the incontinence of Abelard, victim of the noonday devil'.[5]

After some months the couple were caught by Fulbert and required to separate. They continued to meet in secret and soon Heloise wrote to tell Abelard that she was expecting their child. While her uncle was away, Abelard took her from her house and moved her to Brittany to stay with his sister, where she gave birth to a son. Fulbert was enraged by the abduction and Abelard sought to appease him by offering to marry Heloise.

Rather than being pleased with this plan, Heloise herself tried to dissuade Abelard from marriage. To her, Abelard was a glorious

---

1. Abelard and Heloise, 'The Calamities of Peter Abelard', in William Levitan (ed. and tr.), *The Letters and Other Writings* (Indianapolis: Hackett, 2007), p. 10.

2. Ibid., p. 11.

3. Ibid.

4. Ibid., p. 12.

5. Étienne Gilson, *Abelard and Heloise*, tr. L. K. Shook (Ann Arbor: University of Michigan Press, 1960), p. 6.

philosopher, standing in the line of the pagan Seneca or the Christian Jerome, models of the celibacy of the true philosopher and theologian. Abelard himself explained the reasoning common in their day: 'we know that philosophers, and no less scholars of scripture – the ones, that is, who actually want to learn what scripture teaches – have grown strong through their self-restraint'.[6] Heloise thought that marrying him would be an act of cruelty rather than love because it would ruin his reputation and rob him of his status as a self-mastered philosopher. Writing to him years later she persisted in thinking that fornication would have been better than marriage: 'The name of wife may have the advantages of sanctity and safety, but to me the sweeter name will always be *lover* or, if your dignity can bear it, *concubine* or *whore*.'[7] Abelard's audacious solution to this problem was to ask Fulbert to keep the marriage secret. Heloise gave in and the two were secretly married. To preserve the illusion they parted and were able to see each other only occasionally.

Not surprisingly, this arrangement did not satisfy Fulbert's concern for the honour of his house, so he began to spread news of the marriage. When Heloise kept denying it, the tension between them rose, apparently to the point of Fulbert's abusing her. Abelard decided to send his wife away to the safety of the Abbey of Argenteuil, which would also serve to convince others that they were not married. This further angered Fulbert, since it appeared to him that Abelard was now just trying to get rid of his niece. He bribed Abelard's servant, and then with some relatives entered his bedroom by night and castrated him. As Abelard himself described it, they wreaked 'the savage vengeance that has made the whole world shudder – they cut off the parts of my body with which I committed the wrong they complained of.'[8] In shame, guilt and confusion Abelard fled to join the Abbey of Saint-Denys.

The relationship between Abelard and Heloise continued, but in a quite different way. While serving as the Abbot of Saint-Gildas de Rhuys in Brittany, Abelard learned that the nuns of Argenteuil had

---

6. Abelard and Heloise, 'Calamities', in *Letters*, p. 10.

7. First Letter: Heloise to Abelard, in ibid., p. 55 (italics original).

8. 'Calamities', in ibid., p. 18.

been expelled from their monastery, so he gave them his own oratory near Troyes as a new home. Heloise became its first abbess. She and Abelard thence saw each other when he preached for them, but their relationship was now that of a spiritual father and daughter, despite her abiding passion for him.

Disordered love

The story of Abelard and Heloise brings out clearly the flawed nature of fallen human love. The sin of Abelard is obvious: he was a proud man who succumbed to lust and used his position to prey on Heloise. But perhaps the greatest tragedy in the story is the lasting spiritual impact of his assault on the heart of Heloise. While Abelard led her into sin, she seems never to have followed him into the repentance he found after his mutilation. Unlike him, she never accepted the way the Lord had dealt with them. She railed against 'the ungodly savagery of God' and the 'mercilessness of his mercy'.[9] She wrote that she was 'forever unreconciled to his will'.[10] She also continued to dally with the memories of their sinful encounters: 'I see their images even in my sleep. During Holy Mass itself, when prayer should be its purest, unholy fantasies of pleasure so enslave my wretched soul that my devotion is to *them* and not my prayers.'[11]

It is evident from Heloise's own words that Abelard stood in the place of God for her. Gilson comments that in her letters 'one is struck immediately by the omnipresence of Abelard and the total absence of God'.[12] But this is not quite right: God is present in the letters, but only to be accused or to be put firmly in second place to Abelard. She admits that this was her constant choice:

> But in every circumstance throughout my life, as God knows well, I have feared an offense against you more than any offense against him, and I

---

9. Third Letter: Heloise to Abelard, in ibid., p. 74.

10. Ibid., p. 78.

11. Ibid., p. 79 (italics original).

12. Gilson, *Abelard*, p. 88.

have sought to please you more than him. It was your command, not love
for him, that brought me to put on this habit of religion.[13]

In her mind Heloise even reimagined the practices of medieval
religion around Abelard. When she desired to do penance, she was
motivated by a desire to make satisfaction to him for his suffering,
and not to God for her sin:

> I only wish it lay within my power to do a penance worthy of the
> wrong done against *you*, that at least by long contrition I could offer
> some recompense for the wound that you sustained and take upon
> my mind throughout a lifetime of remorse what your body suffered
> in that hour.[14]

Gilson observes that the distress of Heloise on losing Abelard was
'the distress of a worshipper forsaken by her god'.[15]

We have seen that Heloise sinned against God, but it is also
evident that she sinned more specifically against the Son of God.
She replaced Christ with Abelard. She thought that without Abelard
her heart could not exist; but it is in Christ alone that 'all things hold
together' (Col. 1:17). She made Abelard her only lover, but it is Christ
who 'loved the church and gave himself up for her' (Eph. 5:25).
Abelard himself reminds us that human idolatrous love always
fashions other messiahs, other saviours, other lords. After his mutilation, he longed for Heloise to put him aside in favour of God in
Christ. From some of his writings he is known for expressing a
dubious understanding of the cross, but there is no hint of this as
he exhorts her to look to the crucified Christ as her true bridegroom:
'Your brideprice was not his property but himself, for he bought
you and redeemed you with his blood. See what claim he has on you,
look what price he has set on your worth.'[16] He urges her to consider
not his own love but God's love and the value it placed on her: 'you

---

13. Third Letter, in *Letters*, p. 81.
14. Ibid., p. 78 (italics original).
15. Gilson, *Abelard*, p. 93.
16. Fourth Letter: Abelard to Heloise, in *Letters*, p. 100.

are more than the heavens, you are more than the world, whose price was the Creator of the world'.[17]

Selflessness is not necessarily sinless

Despite Abelard's passionate appeals in his letters, there is no hint in their correspondence that God ever did regain his right place in the heart of Heloise. Part of the reason Heloise did not repent was that she thought she was largely innocent in her dealings with Abelard. According to the ancient ethical theory both she and Abelard favoured, the morality of an act is determined solely by its intention: 'For blame does not reside in the action itself but in the disposition of the agent, and justice does not weigh what is done but what is in the heart.'[18] For Abelard and Heloise a good intention was defined by its selflessness. Heloise felt she was innocent because she had always denied herself and sought the good of Abelard. She would have subjected herself even to hell had he told her to:

> But, as God knows, I would have followed you to Vulcan's flames if you commanded it, and without a moment's hesitation I would have gone first. My heart was never my own but was always with you, and now even more, if it is not with you it is nowhere: without you it cannot exist at all.[19]

Unlike the Stoics on whom Abelard and Heloise based their theory, Scripture does not teach that selflessness is the measure of love's quality. Jesus did not just tell us to deny ourselves; he told us to follow him: 'If anyone would come after me, let him deny himself and take up his cross and follow me. For whoever would save his life will lose it, but whoever loses his life for my sake and the gospel's will save it' (Mark 8:34–35).

---

17. Ibid.
18. First Letter, in ibid., p. 59. On their ethics, see Gilson, *Abelard*, pp. 56–60.
19. Ibid., p. 61.

Heloise may have been selfless in her love, but she sinned when she sought Abelard's glory above God's. She gave up her life by taking the veil for Abelard, not for Jesus.

The story of Abelard and Heloise is a tragedy, not a wonderful love story. At first glance there is something moving about the strength of Heloise's devotion, but if we view it with clear sight we will realize that a willingness to follow a man into hell for his own sake is not admirable but abhorrent. We may indeed shed tears for Heloise, but they should be tears of sadness and pity, not wonder. If she did not repent and Abelard did, then, as Gilson notes, her love was also tragically self-defeating: 'It was no longer love, but madness, because in her very excess of love she separated herself forever from the one being she loved.'[20]

The idolatry of disordered love

The tragedy of the beautiful and brilliant Heloise is that her heart locked itself onto Abelard and would never let go, even when God finally placed him beyond her reach. A disordered love-locked heart is a heart in the grip of an idol. To adapt a description from Shakespeare's Juliet, Abelard was the god of her idolatry. The Bible is clear that idolatry is at the heart of sin. That is not to say that sin is only to be understood as idolatry – there are other essential aspects in any definition of sin – but sin is always at least idolatry. When the apostle Paul describes the 'ungodliness and unrighteousness of men' (Rom. 1:18), he analyses it as idolatry: 'Claiming to be wise, they became fools, and exchanged the glory of the immortal God for images resembling mortal man and birds and animals and creeping things' (1:22–23). God responds to idolatry by handing the idolater over to it:

> God gave them up in the lusts of their hearts to impurity, to the dishonouring of their bodies among themselves, because they exchanged the truth about God for a lie and worshipped and served the creature rather than the Creator, who is blessed for ever! Amen. (1:24–25)

---

20. Gilson, *Abelard*, p. 94.

Could there be a more telling description of the love of Abelard and Heloise? They thought themselves wise; they worshipped each other; God handed them over to dishonour their bodies with each other.

For some Heloise's desire for free love and her rebellion against religious norms make her a hero. They have thought her a medieval harbinger of modernity, or at least of the individualism of the Renaissance. But that is a delusion. She was not a hero who broke free; she was a sinner held captive. And in her captivity she was typically human, not peculiarly modern. Her story reveals nothing of the Renaissance or modern heart that is not true of every fallen human heart. In the idolatry of Heloise we see a microcosm of the idolatry of the whole human race. Let us confess it: we see our own idolatry. As Paul's analysis of sin reaches its climax, he indicts not just some particularly bad people, but everyone: 'all have sinned and fall short of the glory of God' (Rom. 3:23).

Our pity for Heloise can never be the pity of condescension, as if we were superior to her. No fallen sinner can look down on another, as Herman Bavinck insists: 'The pride of the self-righteous, the pride of the noble, the self-exaltation of the wise, is, with a view to the human nature which all share alike, absolutely without justification.'[21] If we are set free from our own idolatries, it is not because of our own merit. As Paul continues, we are 'justified by his grace as a gift, through the redemption that is in Christ Jesus' (Rom. 3:24).

I do not tell the story of Heloise because she was unusually sinful, but because she so clearly reveals my fallen loves and yours. Fallen human love is always disordered love. Even the love of a Christian for God is always tainted by disorder in this life. Our very best love for God needs to be cleansed by the blood of Christ. As John Calvin put it, 'by faith alone not only we ourselves but our works as well are justified'.[22]

---

21. Herman Bavinck, *Our Reasonable Faith*, tr. Henry Zylstra (Grand Rapids: Eerdmans, 1956), p. 247.

22. John Calvin, *Institutes of the Christian Religion*, ed. John T. McNeill, tr. Ford Lewis Battles, 2 vols., Library of Christian Classics 20–21 (Philadelphia: Westminster, 1960), 3.17.10, 1:813.

God's perfectly proportioned love

Here is a great contrast between divine and human love. God's love is different from human love because it is always perfectly proportioned. Perfectly proportioned love is love that corresponds to, echoes and reflects the order of reality. As Jonathan Edwards explains, 'true virtue must chiefly consist in love to God; the Being of beings, infinitely the greatest and best of beings'.[23] Love rightly exercised agrees with, rather than fights against, the structure of reality itself, especially the reality of God. It consents to being; it does not war against it. It makes God, the highest good, its highest good.

By contrast, idolatrous love is out of proportion to reality. It refuses being as it is, fighting to deny it. The idolater is like a small child playing with a shape sorter who persistently tries to press the cube into the slot for the cylinder. Human love is disordered because it keeps trying to make created things more than they are and God less than he is.

What does it mean for God's love to be rightly proportioned in regard to himself? It is for him to act in accord with the reality of his own glorious self. It is for him to love himself first, and others within and under his love for himself. Conversely, what would a disorder in God's love look like? It would be for him to act against the truth of reality, to refuse to make himself the highest end of his actions, to make a created thing the highest good in his place. This God does not do, because he cannot sin by setting a creature above himself.

Truly, the Father loves us. He gives his only-begotten Son for us. Truly, the Son lays down his life for us. He is humiliated for us. He puts our pleasure before his pain. In that sense he puts us before himself. But in all this, the Father and the Son seek their own glory as well as our good. When Christ puts us first, it is primarily for his Father's glory. On the eve of his crucifixion for us he prays for his own mutual glorification with the Father, 'Father, the hour has come;

---

23. Jonathan Edwards, *The Nature of True Virtue*, ed. Paul Ramsey, in John E. Smith (ed.), *The Works of Jonathan Edwards* (New Haven: Yale University Press, 1989), 8.550.

glorify your Son that the Son may glorify you' (John 17:1). As he goes to the cross to save us, Jesus seeks to show his love for the Father (John 14:31). Even in saving, God does not give his glory to another (Isa. 48:11). He delights to save us, but not by denying who he is. How absurd it would be to think that he could save us by sinning against himself, by robbing himself of his own glory. He does not set our good above his glory: he acts for both, for his glory first, and under it for our good.

The sinful love of God?

On hearing that God always acts first for his own glory, some respond by asking if he is selfish, as if divine love might itself be sinful and disordered. The opposite is the case: it would be wrong for God to deny who he is, to make a lesser good a higher end than himself. If he did that, he would be acting against the truth of reality, against the truth of his own being. In fact, then he would be sinning: it would be morally wrong for God to fail to act first and foremost for his own glory. This is part of his moral perfection.

When we wonder if God is egotistical, we reveal that we have not grasped the magnitude of the difference between him and his creatures. For a human being to love himself as his own supreme end is always sinful because in reality a human being is never worthy of that position. God is different from us in exactly this regard: he is worthy of being the supreme end of every action, including his own. It is his difference in majesty, glory and worth that makes his self-love not sinful but right and good. It is always right for God to act for his own glory because he is inalienably and infinitely greater than any other being.

Indeed, strictly speaking, God is not on a scale of being that allows us to measure other beings against him. We are being, but he is Being itself. The glorious being of God is shared by the divine persons, who ought to glorify each other. The Father delights to glorify the Son because the Son radiates the glory of the divine being, the Father's own glory. The Son delights to glorify the Father because the Father is the one whose glory he radiates. The Father and Son delight to glorify the Holy Spirit, because he is the Spirit of God and of Christ. And he delights to glorify them, because he is their Spirit. The mutual glory of the three persons must be the delightful, supreme end of the triune God.

Meditation

Behold the perfectly proportioned love of the triune God! Contrast its constant, flawless perfection with the chaotic ocean of loves by which humanity is pushed and pulled, the surging waves of our own loves rushing up from within, the clashing currents of others' loves buffeting us from without. In our natural state we are like drunken men staggering through the rooms of life, upsetting the furniture with our 'love' and leaving disorder in our wake. Like someone with a misshapen figure we bulge in all the wrong places, shrivelled here and distended there.

This is not just the condition of the unbeliever: it is the inclination of the flesh that remains in the believer too. Even though the flesh has been decisively crucified, in its death throes it fights against the Spirit in us (Gal. 5:16–24). The old self will be with us until we die and go to be with Christ. This is why in our thoughts we dwell on the inferior and neglect the superior, why in our words we inflate the lesser and downgrade the greater, and why in our deeds we seize upon the lower and place it above the higher. God should be the ultimate end of all of our actions, but we prefer our own ends and treat God as the means to them. Even as we serve him we seek our own glory, rather than his kingdom and righteousness. The perfectly proportioned love of God is all the more precious to us when we know the disproportion of our own loves.

- *What have been your greatest disproportioned loves?*

Instead of marvelling at God's different love, we all too often attempt to foist our own disordered love onto him. We actually argue that he should be like us, loving himself less than he does and loving us more. We dally with theological systems that demote God from his position as the supreme end and goal of his creation. We are tempted to construct entire accounts of God and his work that are built on the premise that the unadulterated prosperity of every human being must be his supreme concern. Have you ever said, 'But surely if God is love he wouldn't . . .'? And so we dare to tell God what to do. When we do that, we end up speaking not of God, but of god, our own tame idol, with his love refashioned in our likeness and under our control. This god we create prizes not his glory but our independence, not his praise but our ease. And so our theology becomes Big Man theology, in which god is simply a larger projection of our own sinful priorities. 'Evil, be thou my good': like John Milton's Satan we have inverted the definition of right and wrong, replacing God with sinful man.[24]

We beat on a rock with our bare fists. This is not who God has revealed himself to be and we cannot make him what he is not. As the Son reveals the Father we see that God loves in perfect proportion within his own divine life. The Father's love for the Son and the Son's love for the Father are fittingly infinite. In the midst of their life is the Spirit, in whose infinite love the Son offers himself to the Father and is raised from the dead.

Similarly, God's love is perfectly proportioned in his outward acts. God the Father loves us *within* his infinite love for his Son, not as a rival to it. The Father does not introduce disproportion into his love by setting us up in competition with the Son. The Father's love for us leads him to give his Son for us, but the giving of the Son is for the glory of God himself. In John's Gospel Jesus sees the hour of his death as the hour of the Father's glorification (12:27–28). Isaiah prophesied that the Suffering Servant 'shall be high and lifted up, / and shall be exalted' (52:13). Jesus describes to Nicodemus how he would be 'lifted up' on the cross like the bronze serpent in the wilderness (3:14–15). The cross was his exaltation. He lays down his life for us, but that is his glory. God seeks his own triune glory first, and within that he seeks the good of the people he has chosen for glory. This is what his Word tells us he does, and this is what it is right for him to do. Rather than attempting to redefine his love in ways that make it more like our own, we should marvel at it as he has revealed it.

---

24. John Milton, *Paradise Lost*, ed. John Leonard (London: Penguin, 2000), 4.110, p. 76, echoing Isa. 5:20.

- *How are you most tempted to fashion the love of God in the image of
  sinful human love that does not put God first?*

- *How would you most want God to put someone or something other than
  himself before his own glory?*

The contemplation of God's orderly love moves us to reconsider
what we ourselves love first. Often it is hard to tell. Sometimes we
find out how we have loved something only when we lose it, and
we may be pleasantly or unpleasantly surprised. Do we think we
could not live without someone? We should consider the possibility
that that someone may be becoming our love, our life, our very
existence, Abelard to our Heloise. The Bible expects us to experience
anguished grief when we lose someone. At the death of Lazarus
'Jesus wept' (John 11:35). Paul tells us to 'weep with those who weep'
(Rom. 12:15). He does not say that we should not grieve, but only
that we should not grieve like those who have no hope (1 Thess.
4:13). Bitter, deep, wrenching loss is wholly compatible with love for
God. But it will be a loss that, despite anguished struggles along the
way, finally coexists with faith and hope, because it is a loss that
comes in the context of a greater love for the God who remains the
same and can never be lost by his true children. If our loss leads us
finally to abject despair, then we have loved disproportionately. If
we want to know what we love most, we may ask what we look to
for the future: a proper love for God will be evident from our faith
and hope resting in him, not in any thing, man, woman or child.

This does not normally mean giving up all other loves. An ordered
love that puts God first does not conflict with other legitimate loves.
Rather, it provides the only environment in which they can truly
flourish. If in the imagination of our hearts we rip an object from
its proper place under God, and then construct a universe in which
it occupies the supreme place, we have fashioned for our love a
sphere of existence in which it can ultimately only shrivel and die.
If Heloise clung to Abelard, she lost him. The only safe context for
the commandment that we love our neighbour is after the first, that
we love God. It is only by loving things where they truly are in the
order of reality, in subordination to God, that our love for them can
flourish and last for ever. All other environments spell death for our

loves. We should reflect on the fact that by loving created things before the Creator we are signing the death warrant of our love. C. S. Lewis describes the process:

> We may give our human loves the unconditional allegiance which we owe only to God. Then they become like gods: then they become demons. Then they will destroy us, and also destroy themselves. For natural loves that are allowed to become gods do not remain loves. They are still called so, but can become in fact complicated forms of hatred.[25]

Not only that, but loving something in the place of God is harmful to the object of our love itself. Loving something out of its proper place is not truly loving it, since it involves trying to force it to be what it is not. If I love my wife in the place of God, I abuse her because I expect too much of her.

- *Does your love for someone or something spell its sure demise?*

- *How might you be treating others unfairly by putting them in the place of God?*

In examining our loves we should not, therefore, be concerned with *how much* we love, but with *where* we love. Jesus clearly defined and then exemplified the highest possible degree of love for his friends: 'Greater love has no one than this, that someone lay down his life for his friends' (John 15:13). If I lay my life down for someone, then I love them as much as I can: I give for them all that I am, not just things that I own. Jesus commends this kind of love. He does not say that, because it is the highest degree of love, we should reserve it for God alone.

How can this be? How can it be right for us to love a creature with the highest degree of love? Did Jesus in doing this have his love out of proportion? The answer is that the goodness of love is not determined by its quantity, but by its location. I can love rightly in giving my very life for a fellow creature, if I do so in the context

---

25. C. S. Lewis, *The Four Loves* (London: Collins, 1963; repr. 1965), p. 13.

of loving God first. Jesus loved his friends within and under his love for his Father. So too, I can love God and the creature rightly when I love the creature for the sake of God, rather than as a rival to him. If I die saying, 'I do this for you for the glory of God,' then I die rightly. If I die saying, 'I do this for you because you are the be all and end all of my life,' then I sin.

This means that if I want to see whether my love for my wife is disordered, I should not ask how much I love her. I should not ask how intense my love for her feels. I should not ask how much I have given for her. A disordered love is not a love that is too intense, as Lewis explains:

> It remains certainly true that all natural loves can be inordinate. *Inordinate* does not mean 'insufficiently cautious'. Nor does it mean 'too big'. It is not a quantitative term. It is probably impossible to love any human being simply 'too much'.[26]

I should ask instead whether my love for my wife is subordinated within my love for God, whether I am clear that I love her under God, for his sake. As Augustine says to God in his *Confessions*, 'he loves you less who together with you loves something which he does not love for your sake'.[27] If I love my wife for the sake of my love for God, then my love for God is not diminished.

In fact, so long as my love for her is rightly located within my love for God, I should love her with the greatest degree of love, laying my life down for her as Christ did for the church (Eph. 5:25). If I am tired and my wife needs my help, I should put her before myself. If she needs to talk and I am watching television, I should turn it off. If she is sick and I need to care for the children alone, I should protect her rest. On the other hand, I may err in my loves. If I want to spend all the money we have received on an extension, then I have forgotten to give the firstfruits to God. If I want to put our children's sporting success before their involvement at church,

---

26. Ibid., p. 112 (italics original).
27. Augustine, *Confessions*, tr. Henry Chadwick (Oxford: Oxford University Press, 1992), 10.29, p. 202.

then I am loving them before loving God, and am in fact not loving them at all. If I rightly love my wife and children under God, then my love will be properly ordered and will be growing into the likeness of God's love. Lewis identifies the right test: 'the real question is, which (when the alternative comes) do you serve, or choose, or put first? To which claim does your will, in the last resort, yield?'[28]

- *Who or what are your greatest loves? Do you love them for the sake of God?*

Prayer

'Lord God, I know that I do not love you as I should. My loves are so distorted and disordered. My old idols still fight for my heart, and new ones come each day. I constantly struggle to love you first and I often fail. Forgive me for the sake of your Son, who loved you perfectly.

'I delight in the knowledge that your love is flawless, always rightly ordered. I praise you that you always seek your own glory.

'Heavenly Father, I worship you for the way in which you sought in the death of your Son your own glory, his glory and my good.

'Lord Jesus, I praise you that in laying down your life you sought the glory of your Father, your own glory and my good.

'Lord God, may my love for you be my first love. May all my other proper loves flourish within and under it. Help me to love my family, my friends and my neighbours only and always in and under you, for your sake. Amen.'

---

28. Lewis, *Four Loves*, pp. 112–113.

5. THE LOVE OF AN EVER-PRESENT FATHER

The repudiation of family and fatherhood

One of the most remarkable changes in Western culture since the 1960s has been the repudiation of the traditional family, and especially the role of the father within it. I might have said the 'collapse' of the family, but 'repudiation' better captures the strident spirit of the change. What may have begun as embarrassed deviation from the previous norm has become the celebratory embrace of its opposite, even to the extent of claiming that the traditional family is itself the immoral family.

This is not an opinion held only by extremists on the fringe of society who have little voice; it is increasingly the new Establishment position. Jenni Murray has been the regular presenter of *Woman's Hour* since 1987, a programme broadcast six days a week on BBC Radio 4. A skilful and acclaimed journalist, she was nominated Radio Broadcaster of the Year in 1998, received an OBE in 1999, was made a member of the Radio Academy Hall of Fame in 2007, and in 2011 became Dame Jenni Murray. Amid all her professional brilliance, however, she embodies the new radical attitude to marriage. Though she has married twice, Murray long ago repudiated marriage itself as an 'insult'. Her advice is that 'women shouldn't touch it' because it makes a woman a 'legal prostitute'.[1]

Anthony Giddens, formerly Director of the London School of Economics and a close friend and counsellor to Tony Blair, comments that 'the more we learn from historians about traditional families, the more oppressive they often appear to have been'.[2] When the new Blair government issued a document in 1998 entitled *Supporting Families*, the focus was not on traditional families. The previous Conservative government had been mired in controversy when it launched a 'Back to Basics' campaign, and New Labour had no wish to return to what it called back-to-basics 'fundamentalism'.[3] The repudiation of marriage and fatherhood is not limited to the media, academics or politicians: a 1992 Gallup poll found that nearly half the mothers of children aged 0–18 approved of the idea of a woman deciding to have a child outside any kind of 'stable relationship with a man'.[4]

Denying the effects of family breakdown

For a long time the academic world resisted the evidence that the breakdown of the traditional family was causing personal and social problems. Whenever a study suggested that conclusion it was either

---

1. Cited by Norman Dennis and George Erdos, in *Families Without Fatherhood*, 3rd ed. (London: Institute for the Study of Civil Society, 2000), p. 30.
2. Cited in Norman Dennis, 'Beautiful Theories, Brutal Facts: The Welfare State and Sexual Liberation', in David Smith (ed.), *Welfare, Work and Poverty: Lessons from Recent Reforms in the USA and the UK* (London: Institute for the Study of Civil Society, 2000), p. 70.
3. 'Supporting Families', *The National Archives*, http://webarchive. nationalarchives.gov.uk/+/http:/www.nationalarchives.gov.uk/ erorecords/ho/421/2/p2/acu/suppfam.htm#foreword (accessed 20 Nov. 2014).
4. Dennis and Erdos, *Families*, p. 56.

ignored or another explanation was cited to counter it, typically identifying poverty as the cause of problems rather than family breakdown. In popular journalism this line of argument still appears: even while I was writing this chapter a new survey provided further evidence of the harm of divorce, only to be answered in *The Guardian* by Suzanne Moore claiming that poverty might be the cause of hardships and warning us against 'the conservative fetishisation of marriage'.[5]

Despite such thinly rhetorical ripostes, the sheer weight of evidence has forced a growing recognition among serious commentators that the collapse of the traditional family has itself caused a wide variety of grave personal and social problems. In particular, studies on the impact of family breakdown across all classes and degrees of wealth evidence its negative impact. Furthermore, it is clear from historical trends that the rise in personal and social problems does not correlate with a rise in poverty.

This point is made powerfully in a study written by the socialists Norman Dennis and George Erdos. I mention that they write as socialists because it is common to dismiss criticism of social change as right-wing reaction, but Dennis and Erdos are notable for their argument that left-wing thinkers ought to be the proponents of family life, since the left is in other regards more resistant to egotistical individualism than the right.[6] The historical work of Dennis in particular has show that in previous generations poverty did not correlate with social disorder:

> The unemployed men in the North-East of the 1930s, who faced
> far greater material hardship and far more real and lasting uncertainty
> about their futures, did not turn to the 1930s equivalent of ram-raiding
> to pass their time. They kept their culture of family and neighbourly
> mutual aid in good order.[7]

---

5. Suzanne Moore, 'Yes, Divorce Is Bad for Children, but Let's Not Fetishise Marriage at All Costs', *The Guardian*, 24 Nov. 2014.
6. See A. H. Halsey's foreword to Dennis and Erdos, *Families*, p. xiv.
7. As summarized by David G. Green in the 1993 foreword to ibid., p. xi.

Something else beyond poverty needs to happen to turn the poor into criminals on a large scale. Saying that people commit crime because they are poor is insulting to the poor who, despite their difficult circumstances, choose not to riot or steal. There is no necessary connection between poverty and crime: like sin, crime is always a choice. It is a choice more easily made when the traditional pattern of family life and the world view that underpins it have been overturned.

The facts of family breakdown

The facts of family breakdown are clear. By the early 1990s, when Dennis and Erdos wrote their study, around 20 per cent of all families consisted of only one parent, 31 per cent of births were outside marriage, and 150,000 children a year were victims of divorce.[8] Writing in 1996, Dennis reported that there were 1,500,000 households without fathers, making up 20 per cent of all dependent children, twice the number of the mid 1970s.[9]

More recent statistics tell a similar story. In England and Wales in 2010 there were 119,589 divorces.[10] There has been a rise in the divorce rate here since the 1980s: 22 per cent of couples married in 1970 divorced by their fifteenth anniversary, but 33 per cent of couples married in 1995 divorced before theirs. It is significant for gauging the emotional and psychological toll of divorce that the rate is higher in the first twenty years of marriage when children are more likely to be born (the median duration for marriages ending in divorce in 2010 was 11.4 years[11]). The parents of 104,364 children

---

8. Ibid.

9. Dennis, 'Beautiful Theories', p. 47.

10. 'Statistical Bulletin: Divorces in England and Wales 2010: Summary', *Office for National Statistics*, http://www.ons.gov.uk/ons/rel/vsob1/divorces-in-england-and-wales/2010/stb-divorces-2010.html (accessed 13 Aug. 2012).

11. 'Statistical Bulletin: Divorces in England and Wales 2010: Duration of Marriage', *Office for National Statistics*, http://www.ons.gov.uk/ons/rel/vsob1/divorces-in-england-and-wales/2010/stb-divorces-2010.html#tab-duration-of-marriage (accessed 13 Aug. 2012).

aged under 16 divorced in 2010. Of those children, 64 per cent were aged under 11.[12]

It is important to state two qualifications at this point. The first is that while the Bible is clearly against certain patterns of life such as cohabitation and gay marriage, there are cases where it indicates that divorce is permitted, and there will be some instances when it is not just permitted but pastorally necessary. This does not mean that a legitimate divorce will be without painful consequences, but it does remind us that not every married person whose marriage ends is acting wrongly in ending it. My focus here in speaking of the breakdown of the family and of divorce is thus not the small number of legitimate cases that befall even faithful people, but the widespread repudiation of heterosexual marriage as the exclusive standard for family life and the culture of easy divorce.

The second qualification is one stated repeatedly by Dennis and Erdos themselves: the statistics that indicate the deleterious effects of family breakdown are statements of *averages*. This means that they tell us what the average impact of family breakdown is within a group, but not the story of every family or individual in that group, some of whom will have fared much worse and some much better than the average.

The impact of family breakdown

A summary statement of the average impact of the breakdown of fatherhood is shocking. The findings 'show that across the board, physical weight, height, educational achievements, criminality, life and death itself, are on average connected with the presence or absence of a committed father'.[13] Peter Saunders gives the statistics on the impact of family breakdown using the work of Patricia

---

12. 'Statistical Bulletin: Divorces in England and Wales 2010: Children of Divorced Couples', *Office for National Statistics*, http://www.ons.gov.uk/ons/rel/vsob1/divorces-in-england-and-wales/2010/stb-divorces-2010.html#tab-children-of-divorced-couples (accessed 13 Aug. 2012).

13. Dennis and Erdos, *Families*, p. 37.

Morgan.[14] She finds in Britain a mortality rate of babies born to a mother who did not live with the father 68 per cent above those born to married parents. Of children in England in local authority care, 75 per cent were from single-parent households. Divorce doubles the probability that a youth will drift into delinquency, with boys raised in blended, step- or lone-parenting situations twice as likely to appear in court by the time they are 16. Research from the United States shows that males brought up outside a lasting marriage are more than two times more likely to have been in prison by the age of 30.

Saunders also cites *To Have and to Hold*, a 1998 Australian House of Representatives study, which shows that children whose parents separate or divorce 'are two or three times more likely to be *suspended or expelled from school* and are three times more likely to require treatment for *emotional or behavioural problems*'.[15]

The statistics continue to support Dennis's conclusion that 'The consequences for children of the liberation of sex from marriage and the man from the family are severe and incontestable.'[16] The absence of a father is likely to have far-reaching negative effects.

Fighting against creation

Some aspects of family life that have broken down since the 1960s were no doubt merely traditional rather than biblical. Considered in abstraction from the wider world view, specific aspects of the feminist programme align with biblical concerns, such as exposing and prosecuting the horrific abuse of women. Moreover, there were no doubt many outwardly biblically shaped marriages that were in fact nothing of the sort due to hidden marital unfaithfulness and cruelty. Nevertheless, in so far as the traditional family was based on the lifelong, exclusive marriage of one man and one woman, it was the biblical family, and its breakdown has had disastrous personal

---

14. In the afterword to ibid., pp. 96–97.

15. Ibid., p. 97 (italics original).

16. Dennis, 'Beautiful Theories', p. 47.

and social effects. All readers of this book will have seen the impact
of the breakdown on society, families and individuals, and many will
have experienced it first-hand for themselves.

A father jeopardizes his family by his wilful absence because God
has made fathers responsible for families. The adjective 'wilful' is
important here, since the deliberate abandonment of fatherhood
when a family breaks down, especially if it is due to unfaithfulness,
involves rejection for a child in a way that the tragic loss of a loving
father to illness or accident does not. Divorce has not simply stepped
into the shoes of early mortality for the modern family; wilful
absence is uniquely destructive.

We do not live in a universe where we can safely choose to
reinvent the family in whatever shape we wish and inflict or suffer
no consequences. We live in a universe that has been created
by God with a fixed structure for family life that is crucial to the
flourishing of individuals, families and societies. As the apostle Paul
explains, every 'family' or 'fatherhood' (*patria*) in heaven and on
earth is named from God's fatherhood (Eph. 3:15), which means
we can no more easily sidestep fatherhood than we can sidestep
the real world or God himself. God has made each husband the
responsible head of his wife, charged with serving her in selfless,
sacrificial, loving leadership (Eph. 5:22–33), and with bringing
up children 'in the discipline and instruction of the Lord' (Eph.
6:4). The created order is inescapable, so that even fugitive fathers
cannot avoid impacting their families, a point made vividly by
Douglas Wilson:

> Because the husband is head of the wife, he finds himself in a position
> of *inescapable leadership*. He cannot successfully refuse to lead. If he
> attempts to abdicate in some way, he may, through his rebellion, lead
> poorly. But no matter what he does, or where he goes, he does so as the
> head of his wife. This is how God designed marriage. He has created us
> as male and female in such a way as to ensure that men will always be
> dominant in marriage. If the husband is godly, then that dominance
> will not be harsh; it will be characterized by the same self-sacrificial love
> demonstrated by our Lord – *Dominus* – at the cross. If a husband tries
> to run away from his headship, that abdication will dominate the home.
> If he catches a plane to the other side of the country, and stays there,

he will dominate in and by his absence. How many children have grown up in a home *dominated* by the empty chair at the table?[17]

Who are the fatherless?

The anxious conservative can easily become preoccupied by the modern tragedy of family breakdown, but we need to remember that it pales into insignificance against the backdrop of the underlying universal tragedy of the human race from which it ultimately springs. According to the Bible, every human being is conceived fatherless. Adam was created as the 'son of God' (Luke 3:38), but his fall into sin alienated him from his Father. When God came looking for him, Adam hid (Gen. 3:8). His own withdrawal was then echoed in the punishment for sin imposed upon him and his children: the man who hid from God was now expelled from the garden where God walked and could be met.

There remains a very general sense in which God 'fathers' every human being as creator. The apostle Paul quotes approvingly the pagan poet Aratus' description of all people as God's offspring (Acts 17:28–29). Every human being knows something of the fatherhood of God simply by being created, and from his providential care. Nonetheless, the same apostle tells the Ephesians that they were by nature not children of God but 'children of wrath, like the rest of mankind' (Eph. 2:3). Every human individual is conceived without a divine Father. Apart from the grace of God every human being after Adam except Jesus himself is by nature in a state of fatherlessness. If we want to explain the problems of society, this deeper kind of fatherlessness is inestimably more significant than even the absence of a human father. This is why prior to the collapse of the traditional family human history was not exactly a picture of universal health and happiness.

---

17. Douglas Wilson, *Reforming Marriage*, 2nd ed. (Moscow, Idaho: Canon, 2005), p. 24 (italics original).

A Father for the fatherless

Every human being begins without a divine father, and for many in our times that absence is compounded by the absence of a human father. To such fatherless people as we all are, the gospel brings the good news of a divine Father who lovingly seeks us. He is the shepherd looking for the lost sheep, the father for his rebellious son: 'while he was still a long way off, his father saw him and felt compassion, and ran and embraced him and kissed him' (Luke 15:20). The return of his children is enabled by God himself in his sovereign power: 'No one can come to me unless the Father who sent me draws him' (John 6:44).

Sinclair Ferguson describes sonship as '*the apex of creation and the goal of redemption*'.[18] Created Adam was a son of God, and into that status Israel was redeemed. The fatherhood of God and sonship of his people are clearly revealed in the events of the exodus from Egypt. Moses was told to speak to Pharaoh for God: 'Israel is my firstborn son, and I say to you, "Let my son go that he may serve me." If you refuse to let him go, behold, I will kill your firstborn son' (Exod. 4:22–23). Moses later reminded the Hebrews that God had carried them through the wilderness 'as a man carries his son' (Deut. 1:31). Hosea recalls the love of God for his child in bringing him out of Egypt (11:1). The law against rituals for the dead such as self-cutting is prefaced with the words 'You are the sons of the LORD your God' (Deut. 14:1). In the Psalms David likens the compassion of God to the compassion of a father for his children (103:13). But the fatherhood of God could also be the basis of prophetic warnings:

> Children have I reared and brought up,
>   but they have rebelled against me.
> (Isa. 1:2–3)

Even with this clear vein of evidence, there are few references to God as Father in the Old Testament compared to the more than

---

18. Sinclair Ferguson, *Children of the Living God* (Edinburgh: Banner of Truth Trust, 1989; repr. 2011), p. 6 (italics original).

two hundred references in the New.[19] This is because in the New Testament the Son of God himself comes. Jesus alone is the eternal Son of the Father, but by being joined to him we come to share in his status of sonship. He has a natural sonship, but ours is derived from and dependent upon him. God is our Father because he is first the Father of the Son.

A Father by regeneration and adoption

In the language of the New Testament we enter the family of God by new birth and by adoption. The Holy Spirit uses both images for the way in which we become God's children, as if to give us a double assurance of his love. Jesus speaks in John's Gospel of how we become children of God by means of being born again. John Murray gives a stirring definition of this act of regeneration:

> God effects a change which is radical and all-pervasive, a change which cannot be explained in terms of any combination, permutation, or accumulation of human resources, a change which is nothing less than a new creation by him who calls the things that be not as though they were, who spake and it was done, who commanded and it stood fast. This, in a word, is regeneration.[20]

This stupendous work occurs only by the sovereign will of the Holy Spirit, who like the wind 'blows where it wishes' and puts a new heart and spirit within those born again (John 3:8; Ezek. 36:26).

Paul speaks several times in key passages of how we are adopted into God the Father's family. While the language of John suggests a newly recreated nature, the word used by Paul (*huiothesia*) describes a new legal status given to the child of God. The Roman concept of adoption, with which his readers would have been familiar, entailed a decisive break with the old status and joining a new family

---

19. Ferguson gives the number in ibid., p. xi.
20. John Murray, *Redemption Accomplished and Applied* (Edinburgh: Banner of Truth Trust, 1961), p. 96.

under a new *paterfamilias*. All obligations and debts were cancelled and new obligations formed.

We see the momentous nature of the transition in the imagery Paul uses in Romans. Previously sin had been our king reigning over us (Rom. 6:12), our general commanding the use of our members (*hopla*, 'weapons'; 6:13), our master exercising dominion over us (6:14) and our employer paying the wages of sin in our death (6:23).[21] But God has predestined us to be 'conformed to the image of his Son' (8:29), he has given us the 'Spirit of adoption as sons, by whom we cry, "Abba! Father!"' (8:15) and we await the final outworking of our adoption, 'the redemption of our bodies' (8:23).

Whereas some classical Reformed writers subsumed adoption under justification (e.g. Francis Turretin[22]), it is clear that while both are legal images, the privileges of adoption are distinct from and additional to those of justification: sonship requires, but is not reducible to, righteousness. Indeed, adoption is really the supreme blessing that rests upon but goes beyond the new status of the believer as righteous in Christ. It is, as Murray puts it, 'the apex of grace and privilege'.[23]

An ever-present Father

The love of God for the believer is the love of the Father for his sons, regenerated and adopted in his Son. Whereas our world is full of fathers who have abandoned their children, our heavenly Father will never leave his children. God is not just a Father to us; he is an ever-present Father.

We can see this clearly by combining our thoughts about the love of the Father with the biblical doctrine of God's omnipresence, his being present everywhere and always. In Psalm 139 David testifies to the omnipresence of God:

---

21. Paul's imagery is summarized like this by Ferguson in *Children*, p. 87.
22. See his *Institutes of Elenctic Theology*, ed. James T. Dennison, tr. George Musgrave Giger, 3 vols. (Phillipsburg: P. & R., 1992–7), 16.6.1, 2:666.
23. Murray, *Redemption*, p. 134.

> Where shall I go from your Spirit?
>> Or where shall I flee from your presence?
> If I ascend to heaven, you are there!
>> If I make my bed in Sheol, you are there!
> If I take the wings of the morning
>> and dwell in the uttermost parts of the sea,
> even there your hand shall lead me,
>> and your right hand shall hold me.
> (vv. 7–10)

So too God says through the prophet Jeremiah, 'Do I not fill heaven and earth?' (Jer. 23:24).

As with his other attributes, we need to understand the omnipresence of God analogically: his presence is at once like and unlike other presences. Things, Stephen Charnock explains, are said to be present in one of three ways. Things like people are present in bodily form in just one place. Spirits like angels are also present in one place, but they are not present bodily. God alone is present everywhere as spirit: 'He is from the height of the heavens to the bottom of the deeps, in every point of the world, and in the whole circle of it, yet not limited by it, but beyond it.'[24] While God is present in all creation, he is not contained by it, but is infinitely beyond it, even beyond heaven itself: 'heaven and the highest heaven cannot contain you' (1 Kgs 8:27). As Charnock explains, heaven is 'the court of his majestical presence, but not the prison of his essence'.[25]

Perhaps one of the most mysterious aspects of God's presence is that he is wholly present everywhere. He is not stretched out so that part of him is present here while part of him is elsewhere, because he has no parts. A very tall man may have his toes on the floor and his head pressed against the ceiling. We might say he is present to both floor and ceiling, but he is not *wholly* present to both; he achieves his presence in two places by stretching out his body

---

24. Stephen Charnock, *The Existence and Attributes of God* (Grand Rapids: Baker, 1996; repr. 2000), 1.367–368.
25. Ibid. 1.385.

and distributing its parts. God, without body or parts, is present in his entirety everywhere. Nor is God present by permeating himself through the matter of the universe, for example by spreading himself out through the gaps between molecules. As God, he is not present materially, so his omnipresence does not mean that he mixes himself with created stuff. Nor is he present by multiplying his essence again and again, copying himself out until he fills all of space, as a child might repeat a pattern to fill a page. No, God is in and beyond all places totally.[26]

So far we have considered the presence of God as God, in his divine essence. God is present in the same way to all as far as the simple presence of his essence is concerned, but there are further ways in which the Bible speaks of his being present that are not the same for all. There are different ways in which God may be present. This explains why some texts such as Psalm 139 speak of his omnipresence, while others speak of his withdrawing his presence, most famously the cry of dereliction 'why have you forsaken me?' (Ps. 22:1; Mark 15:34). Charnock explains the different ways in which God may be thought of as present:

> There are several manifestations of his presence; he hath a presence of glory in heaven, whereby he comforts the saints; a presence of wrath in hell, whereby he torments the damned; in heaven he is a God spreading his beams of light; in hell, a God distributing his strokes of justice; by the one he fills heaven; by the other he fills hell; by his providence and essence he fills both heaven and earth.[27]

God is not more present to one person than another by essence, but he is present differently in other ways: 'He is equally present with the damned and the blessed, as he is an infinite Being, but not in regard of his goodness and grace.'[28]

As God, the Son is omnipresent in his divine essence. As man, the same Son is present in just one place at a time, now at the right

---

26. Charnock makes these points in ibid. 1.374–375.

27. Ibid. 1.370.

28. Ibid. 1.373.

hand of God the Father (Heb. 1:3). In his speech in Acts 7 Stephen defends himself from the charge that he denounced the temple. He does not deny that the temple was the dwelling place of God, but he does recount various ways in which God had met his people in other places before and beyond the temple, even on Gentile ground in Mesopotamia, Egypt and the wilderness. Towards the end of his speech Stephen sees heaven itself opened and Christ standing at the right hand of the Father. He is the new temple (John 2:18–22), the dwelling place of God, now in the heavenly home of God's glory. There is a new place where God dwells, and it is in the heavenly Jesus.

Given this, how could Jesus himself promise his disciples, 'I am with you always, to the end of the age' (Matt. 28:20)? If he is in heaven and heaven is the place of glory, how can he be with us here below in the goodness and grace of his human nature? John Calvin puts the answer beautifully: 'the coming of the Spirit and the ascent of Christ are antithetical'.[29] When Christ ascends, he sends the Holy Spirit down to be with us. Because the Spirit is his Spirit, the Spirit of Christ (Rom. 8:9), he mediates Christ's presence to us. The Son is with us to the end of the age by the Spirit.

Does this then mean that we always have our Brother with us, but not our Father? Do we have only the goodness and grace of the Son with us, but not the goodness and grace of the Father? Is God the Father ever-present with us only in his essence (as he is present even to the lost), but not as our loving *Father*? This does not follow, because as the Son is present in his goodness and grace by the Spirit, so the Father is present in his goodness and grace by the Son. The Spirit makes the Son present to us, and in doing that makes the Father present to us as well, because the Father is in the Son and the Son is in the Father (John 14:10). The persons of the God-head indwell one another, so that by having the Son in us by the Spirit we have the Father in us by the Son. Our Brother and Father together come to dwell in us: 'If anyone loves me, he will keep my

---

29. John Calvin, *Institutes of the Christian Religion*, ed. John T. McNeill, tr. Ford Lewis Battles, 2 vols., Library of Christian Classics 20–21 (Philadelphia: Westminster, 1960), 4.17.26, 2.1393.

word, and my Father will love him, and we will come to him and make our home with him' (John 14:23). Because the Son has promised us that he will never leave, we have the same assurance from the Father who is in him.

Meditation

A Roman slave adopted by his master presumably had an interest in his own history and in the act of adoption itself, but his awareness of the riches of his new life came from knowing his new family. So too with the believer: if we wish to sound the wonders of adoption, then we need primarily to meditate not on ourselves as adoptees or on the adoptive act itself, but on our new family, the Brother we now have and the Father we now know through him. We are brothers of the Son of God and children of his heavenly Father.

We can understand what it means to be a son of the Father by looking at how the Father relates to his Son. God's first words to his Son in the Gospels at his baptism are words of delight: 'You are my beloved Son; with you I am well pleased' (Mark 1:11). What is true of the head (Jesus) is true of the body (the church). The Father's words to the Son are his words to the Son's brothers, the Father's adopted children: he delights in us. By looking at his relationship to the Son, you see how the Father delights in you.

The Son's baptism was a foretaste of his death; he later spoke of his death as a baptism (Mark 10:38), and he was baptized not for the forgiveness of his own sins (since he had none), but as a sign that he stood with us, that he had come to take our sins upon himself. It is no surprise then that the Father loved the Son at his baptism and in his death. Though the Father abhorred the work of those dishonouring Jesus by crucifying him, he loved the Son for his obedient self-offering: 'For this reason the Father loves me, because I lay down my life that I may take it up again' (John 10:17). The Father's love for the Son is his love for the Son's brothers, the Father's adopted children: he loves us. See how the Father loves you!

Following his work of making purification for sins on the cross, Jesus was 'appointed the heir of all things' (Heb. 1:2).[30] This is one of the seven ways in which the writer to the Hebrews highlights the Son's uniqueness (1:1–4), so it is all the more striking when we read elsewhere that we are 'heirs of God and fellow heirs with Christ' (Rom. 8:17). Many of the riches God has for us are ours now: the Father 'has blessed us in Christ with every spiritual blessing in the heavenly places' (Eph. 1:3). Others, especially our material riches, will wait until the new earth. The Father's inheritance for the Son is his inheritance for the Son's brothers, the Father's adopted children: we will receive what he has received. See the inheritance the Father has given you!

When Paul addressed the boastful factionalism of the Corinthian church, he did not tell the Corinthians that they did not have Paul or Apollos or Cephas, in whom they boasted. As well as telling them to boast in Christ alone (1 Cor. 1:31), he told them that their boasting was ridiculous because it actually set its sights too low. Rather than just having their favourite leader, they in fact had all things: 'let no one boast in men. For all things are yours, whether Paul or Apollos or Cephas or the world or life or death or the present or the future – all are yours, and you are Christ's, and Christ is God's' (1 Cor. 3:21–23). See the logic here: the believer has what is Christ's and Christ has what is God's, which is all things. Boasting in Paul or Apollos or Cephas is too small a thing for the Christian who has everything in Christ. The Father delights in the Son, loves the Son and gives the Son all things; therefore, he delights in us, loves us and has given us all things.

- *Dwell on the delight, love and inheritance that is yours as a child of God.*

- *Do you struggle with a sense of what you do not have, with comparing your own prosperity to that of others who have more? Consider what you have in Christ.*

---

30. For this reading of the timing of the appointment, see Peter T. O'Brien, *The Letter to the Hebrews* (Grand Rapids: Eerdmans; Nottingham: Apollos, 2010), p. 52.

Does the glorious truth of the ever-present Father and of our great inheritance mean that we can expect to live a life prosperous in every way here and now? This is a view that has gripped much of the global church. We need to be careful lest we deceive ourselves into thinking that life for the children of God will be easy. If we think that God has promised us prosperity, then we may well later be stunned into unbelief when something hard happens to us, and round on God for his broken promise.

One of the things the Bible tells us about the Father's love is that it is a love that disciplines us for our own good, and is, therefore, entirely compatible with hardship befalling us, even what appears humanly speaking to be disaster. God is like human fathers who do not allow their straying children to go unchecked, only his discipline is perfect: 'they disciplined us for a short time as it seemed best to them, but he disciplines us for our good, that we may share his holiness' (Heb. 12:10). In the context of this verse the main type of disciplinary suffering seems to be persecution, but other passages suggest a broader definition of suffering in general, including illness and death and the ongoing struggle against sin (e.g. Rom. 7:7–25; 1 Cor. 11:27–32; 2 Cor. 4:7–18). A Christian may face the unexpected death of a parent, of a husband or wife, of a tiny, precious baby from congenital disease, long years of degenerative illness, unwanted singleness or childlessness, unemployment and poverty, the relentless war of attrition against besetting temptations; the list goes on and on.

Why would the Father allow this for his sons? Because it was the path of even his infinitely precious only-begotten Son. The writer to the Hebrews is clear that Christians are to suffer because Jesus suffered: 'Consider him who endured from sinners such hostility against himself, so that you may not grow weary or fainthearted' (12:3). Even Christ learned obedience through his sufferings (Heb. 5:8); how much more the sinful believer can learn through his. Calvin once wrote to persecuted Christians in his home country France explaining that suffering is a consequence of the believer's union with Christ. If we are children of God in Christ, then we must suffer as he did: 'above all by sufferings he wishes us to be conformed to the image of his Son, as it is fitting that there should be conformity between the head and the members'.[31] Calvin, who suffered much in his own life in many ways, found refusal of this truth hard to comprehend: 'It is horrible that those who call themselves Christians should be so stupid, or rather brutalized, as to renounce Jesus Christ as soon as he displays his cross.'[32] If Christ is our Brother, we should expect the cross. That is what the Father's love meant for him, and it is what it will mean for us.

God does not abandon us when he disciplines us. In the midst of the troubles of life that will sooner or later hem us in, the Father will always be with us. And because he is the ever-present Father, we know there is nowhere trouble can take us that is beyond his reach to help. Hear this encouraging word from Charnock: 'He that is the sanctuary of his people in all calamities, is more present with them to support them, than their adversaries can be present with them to afflict them.'[33] Here is a tonic for us in the face of the trials of the Christian life: the love of our heavenly Father will always be the nearest thing to us.

Here too is the good news of the gospel to be proclaimed to all men, women and children who are conceived cut off from the heavenly Father by sin: our days of hiring ourselves out to feed unclean pigs and longing to eat their food, of wallowing in father-lessness, can be over. God will have us back as our Father again, and his love will always be with us, even as we walk through the valley of the shadow of death (Ps. 23:4). And here is perhaps a particular tonic for the soul of modern men, women and children who have experienced wilful abandonment by an earthly father. The pain inflicted on a child by infidelity runs very deep and long through a life, but the grace of God abounds to meet it. Mental struggles with anxiety and despair may be near, but God the Father is always nearer.

- *What kind of a life do you expect from your heavenly Father?*

---

31. John Calvin, *Selected Works of John Calvin: Tracts and Letters*, ed. Henry Beveridge and Jules Bonnet (Grand Rapids: Baker Book House, 1983), 7.84–85.
32. Ibid. 7.86.
33. Charnock, *Existence and Attributes* 1.400.

- *Have you been surprised when you have encountered hardship?*

- *What does your suffering say about how the Father views you?*

The risk of reading a book like this on your own (as most readers will) is that it encourages you in your individualism: you read about God's love for *you* and *your* relationship to him. Meditating on your status as a child of God is a good point at which to lay to rest individualistic conceptions of the Christian life and to dwell on the corporate nature of our walk with the Lord Jesus. Of course we need to come to him as individuals, but when we come to him we become part of his family. We have one Brother, but many brothers. God predestined us 'to be conformed to the image of his Son, in order that he might be the firstborn among many brothers' (Rom. 8:29). The Christian life is not about the Father, the Son and *me*. It is about the Father of the church and the firstborn Brother among many brothers. We have a new Father, and because of that we have a new family. Our new family is both a privilege and a responsibility. We are never to be without earthly love and support, and we are always to offer it to others.

- *Are there ways in which you have an individualistic view of your Christian life?*

- *How have you known the love and support of brothers and sisters in the church?*

- *Where is your commitment to them evident?*

Prayer

'Heavenly Father, I come to you naturally fatherless, cut off by sin and wandering alone. I thank you that you have searched for me, that you have run towards me to embrace me, that you have adopted me as your child by joining me to your most precious Son.

'I praise you for the new nature that you have given me by the regenerative work of your Holy Spirit, and for the status you have conferred on me as your adopted child.

'I thank you that you are always with me in your divine essence, but all the more that you are with me by your Son and your Spirit, and that you have promised never to leave.

'Would you open my eyes to the wonderful truth that you delight in me, love me, and have made me a fellow heir with your Son. Keep me from boasting in trivial possessions, mindful of all that is mine in Christ.

'Help me to have realistic expectations of life in this fallen world. Forgive me for the ways in which I have misread your hand of discipline. Open my eyes to see in my hardships signs of your fatherly love, to discern the holiness you would grow in me through suffering.

'Please forgive me for the ways in which I am too focused on myself and my own walk with you. Keep me from selfish individualism. Remind me of my family, my brothers and sisters, and enable me to be a blessing to them. In Jesus' name. Amen.'

6. LOVE THAT DOES NOT NEED THE LOVED

The other half

Some husbands and wives are very similar to each other. They have the same type of personality, the same interests and share the same friends. If they have strengths, their strengths are magnified by being joined. They become exceptional at some ways of living. If they have weaknesses, their weaknesses too may be multiplied as they fail to spot them and spur one another on in them as much as in their strengths. It is easy to see why we might be attracted to someone like us, to our own likeness, since we probably prize the things we are good at and esteem them in others too.

On the other hand, it is obvious why we might be attracted to someone different, since we may be acutely aware of our own deficiencies and marvel at someone who excels in the areas where we fail. For example, someone who is emotionally tough and very good at keeping going in a crisis where resilience is required may be attracted to someone who shows more sensitivity and awareness towards a friend who is struggling. The husband who talks too much may admire the reticence of his quieter wife, wishing that he could bite his lip more often and listen more patiently without interrupting.

The marriages of couples who are similar may flourish because the husband and wife react in the same ways and agree on most things, rarely coming to loggerheads. Those who are different may flourish because the couple's personalities fit each other like the differently shaped pieces of a jigsaw puzzle to produce a rounded whole.

The idea of partners completing each other by supplying what they lack is reflected in the ancient Greek theory that every individual is half of an original person. In Plato's dialogue *The Symposium* Aristophanes explains that the first humans were actually spherical, with four hands, four legs and two faces. If they were in a hurry, they could stick out all eight limbs and run by spinning round and round, like someone doing cartwheels. When these early humans attacked the gods, Zeus decided to cut them all in half, as one might cut an apple or an egg in half. This would leave them much slower, able to run only on two legs, and Zeus warned that if they continued to be troublesome he would then cut them in half again so that they could only hop! Having cut all the spherical humans in half, he tasked Apollo to do some tidying up to fashion them into the shape we now have. This left us weaker, but also greater in number and, therefore, more useful to the gods. Aristophanes uses this theory to explain love, the subject of the dialogue:

> Man's original body having been thus cut in two, each half yearned for
> the half from which it had been severed. When they met they threw their
> arms round one another and embraced, in their longing to grow together
> again, and they perished of hunger and general neglect of their concerns,
> because they would not do anything apart.[1]

For Plato, this story explained not only love, but also sexuality, since the original human beings might have been made up of not just man and woman, but also two men or two women, thus producing

---

1. Plato, *The Symposium*, tr. Walter Hamilton (London: Penguin, 1951), p. 61.

same-sex couples. At this point, the story of course conflicts with the biblical account in Genesis 1 – 2 of the original human pair being male and female, a passage appealed to by Jesus himself (Matt. 19:3–12). Nevertheless, the image of originally spherical human beings seeking their 'other halves' vividly expresses what many people feel in a relationship – that it is in relationship with another person that they become complete, that they find what they lack in another.

Doubtless there are many things wrong with such an idea, not least of all the fact that the perfect man, the Lord Jesus, was never in such a relationship with another human individual (though there is much to be said about the church being his bride). There is nothing humanly incomplete in a single person. There is, however, a sense in which for the work that he was given to do, Adam needed Eve to complete him. The biblical account is not concerned with the matching of personality traits; the idea is not that Eve augmented Adam because they had certain traits that were better together. The biblical picture of marriage certainly includes the idea of physical complementarity for the purpose of procreation, which in turn enables the subduing of the earth by multiplication (Gen. 1:26–28). But Eve was necessary for Adam for far more than reproductive purposes.

It was not good for Adam to be alone primarily from the perspective of the task he had been given. Adam needed Eve and Eve needed Adam because of their divinely defined gender roles, which together enabled them to pursue their work of subduing the earth. In the male–female marriage relationship the husband finds in his wife what he is not, and she finds in him what she is not, for their divinely given work. He is her 'head' (Eph. 5:23), a term indicating his great responsibility in subduing the earth, and she is his 'helper' (Gen. 2:18), indicating great dignity, as we see when it is used of God in his relation to Israel (Ps. 115:9–11). In their divinely ordered relationship husband and wife depend on each other for being what they are as a married couple, both physically and in their work. In this way marriage reveals that when we love, we are indeed seeking what we do not have in ourselves. The husband and wife need each other to bring what they themselves cannot bring to their marriage. Their difference is crucial to their love.

We are not God's other half

Here is a point of great contrast with the love of God. God does not look for what he lacks in his beloved, because he lacks nothing. He creates things that reflect the perfection he already has, rather than things that bring him more perfection. He creates out of the superabundance of his own being, not out of any lack. He is the Alpha and Omega, the beginning and the end (said by God in Rev. 1:8, and by Christ in Rev. 1:17), so he encompasses all time as its source and purpose. He is the immortal one (1 Tim. 1:17), so he possesses immortal life. He is the I AM (Exod. 3:14), so he is self-existent and self-determining. God has his being and will from himself and no other. This attribute of God, known technically as his 'aseity' (from the Latin *a se*, 'from himself'), comes out very clearly when in Psalm 50 God attacks the common ancient idea that sacrifices are food for the hungry gods:

> I will not accept a bull from your house
> > or goats from your folds.
> For every beast of the forest is mine,
> > the cattle on a thousand hills.
> I know all the birds of the hills,
> > and all that moves in the field is mine.
> If I were hungry, I would not tell you,
> > for the world and its fullness are mine.
> Do I eat the flesh of bulls
> > or drink the blood of goats?
> Offer to God a sacrifice of thanksgiving,
> > and perform your vows to the Most High,
> and call upon me in the day of trouble;
> > I will deliver you, and you shall glorify me.
> (vv. 9–15)

Similarly, when the apostle Paul saw the altars of the Athenians, he told them:

> The God who made the world and everything in it, being Lord of heaven
> and earth, does not live in temples made by man, nor is he served by

human hands, as though he needed anything, since he himself gives to all mankind life and breath and everything. (Acts 17:24–25)

Because God does not create things to complete himself, he does not love from any need for his beloved. He does not depend on the creation to be who he is or to do what he does. As C. S. Lewis puts it, 'In God there is no hunger that needs to be filled, only plenteous-ness that desires to give.'[2] Creation does not make God into anything he was not already, as if he were an imperfect being in the process of becoming. This vitally important idea merits further reflection. Two explanatory points will take us deeper into it.

The diversity of creation

The first point concerns God's attitude to diversity. It is tempting to think that he creates the world in order to expand the range of reality, to add perfections that are not already present in him. However, this cannot be true, which may then leave us wondering why the creation does contain such diversity. If God is not filling gaps, what is he doing?

God evidently does love diversity. He creates extraordinary variety in the seen and unseen realms of creation. We should stand in awed silence before the sheer unimaginable richness of even those parts of the created universe we can see. Think of the different types of trees: tall and short, red and green, thick and thin, gnarled and spindly. Consider the animals: dangerous and placid, hooting and silent, vivid and camouflaged, dainty and blundering. When we hear the statistics describing the unseen extent of the universe and its contents, we can but gasp. It is filled with mysteries, from black holes to subatomic particles.

God's love for diversity is seen not only in his creative but also his redemptive work, for example in his plan to draw all nations to Christ, in bringing the gospel to 'Parthians and Medes and Elamites and residents of Mesopotamia, Judea and Cappadocia, Pontus and

---

2. C. S. Lewis, *The Four Loves* (London: Collins, 1963; repr. 1965), p. 116.

Asia, Phrygia and Pamphylia, Egypt and the parts of Libya belonging to Cyrene, and visitors from Rome, both Jews and proselytes, Cretans and Arabians' (Acts 2:9–11), through Jerusalem, Judaea, Samaria 'and to the end of the earth' (Acts 1:8). His purpose embraces every nation, tribe, people and language (Rev. 7:9). Reading this book in the language of English, here and now, you yourself are a sign of God's love for diversity.

The more we appreciate the extraordinary richness of the created and redeemed world, the more we may wonder why God has designed it like this if he does not need it. As a child growing up in England in the 1970s I had never eaten papaya or guava or star fruit. When we moved to Hong Kong in 1982, I tasted these fruits for the first time. I loved the diversity of the new flavours and textures because I had not experienced them before. But God does not love diversity because it brings him something he does not already have. He does not need the rich life of creation because he himself lacks its richness. The necessity runs the other way: creation needs its rich life because its creator already has the richest life. If the creation is to reflect God properly, then it needs to have a rich diversity, for the very reason that his divine life is already so rich and full.

God made the world to reveal his glory. That is its purpose, as Scripture repeatedly attests. When God prophesied the gathering of his scattered people through Isaiah, he described them as those 'created for my glory' (Isa. 43:7). As Jesus looked towards the hour of the cross, he prayed 'Father, glorify your name' (John 12:28). Paul tells the Corinthians to 'do all to the glory of God' (1 Cor. 10:31). The purpose of creation is to glorify God. One of the ways in which it does this is by reflecting the glory God himself already has.

God is not like a jigsaw with several pieces missing. Without some of its pieces a jigsaw is frustratingly flawed. To be complete it needs the missing pieces. The different pieces are necessary to fill the gaps in the jigsaw, to make up for what it lacks. God does not need the diversity in his creation to complete him. Instead, imagine a finished jigsaw with every piece present and a mirror in which you can see a reflection of it. The mirror reflects the diversity already present in the jigsaw and does not add anything new to the jigsaw itself. This is a better picture of the relationship between God and his creation. God is already complete, and the world reflects the richness of who he already is. God makes and redeems a world rich in diversity as an outpouring of his already full glory.

The Trinity does not mean God has needs

The second explanatory point concerns the Trinity and God's love for diversity. We have seen that God loves the diversity of creation outside himself. The doctrine of the Trinity, however, reveals that God also loves the difference within his own divine life.

God's own inner love, his intra-trinitarian love, involves his loving difference. The Father loves a distinct person from himself when he loves the Son. And the Father loves the Son *for* his difference, for his obedient sonship in going to the cross (John 10:17). There is a real love for difference in God. This does not of course mean that there is diversity of being or essence in God as there is in the creation: the Son differs in personhood from the Father, not in being. But God loves the distinctions in his own inner life.

By loving the Son, is the Father captured by someone independent of him? Does he lose his aseity? This does not follow, because the love of the Father for the Son is not love for a different being from himself. In loving the Son the Father loves the radiance of his own glory, not someone outside himself. The Father in loving the Son loves one who is in himself and in whom he is: 'I am in the Father and the Father is in me' (John 14:11). Hilary of Poitiers has a wonderful reflection on this mysterious mutual indwelling:

> It seems impossible that one object should be both within and without another, or that (since it is laid down that the Beings of whom we are treating, though They do not dwell apart, retain their separate existence and condition) these Beings can reciprocally contain One Another, so that One should permanently envelope, and also be permanently enveloped by, the Other, whom yet He envelopes.

How, Hilary asks, can the Father be inside the Son and at the same time the Son be inside the Father? Of course part of the answer lies in remembering that we are not speaking about a physical inhabitation here, as if the mutual indwelling of the persons implied something like a letter being folded inside its envelope and the envelope at the same time being folded inside the letter. Nevertheless, this clarification will take us only so far; it does not explain the mystery. As Hilary concludes, 'what man cannot understand, God can be'.[3] Though we cannot fathom it, the mutual indwelling of the divine persons shows that in loving the difference of his Son the Father does not love what is not God. The necessarily trinitarian love of God for his own difference does not conflict with his aseity.

Meditation

A summary of these somewhat dense doctrinal reflections may help as we move to meditation. I have argued that God does not love us because he needs us to complement what he lacks in his own life. He creates the diversity among the things he has made because it enables them to reflect all the richness of his own life. God also loves the difference within his own triune life, but this does not mean he is captured by anyone outside himself.

Perhaps the picture of God as the lover who does not need us leaves us uncomfortable or dissatisfied. We all enjoy feeling we are needed by others. It can be very gratifying to be told, 'I could not cope without you,' to feel that someone depends on us. It is easy to confuse this feeling of being needed with the reality of being loved, but they are very different. God does not need us, but he does love us with the greatest love. His love is uncaused by anything we might give to him. We do not make the smallest contribution to who he is. We add absolutely nothing to him.

The fact that God does not need us actually makes his love for us all the more extraordinary. This difference between divine and human love does not lessen his love; it magnifies it. If God were an idol who needed us to bring him food, then we might easily think

---

3. Hilary of Poitiers, *On the Trinity*, in Philip Schaff and Henry Wace (eds.), *Nicene and Post-Nicene Fathers*, second series, 14 vols. (Buffalo: Christian Literature, 1886–90; repr. Peabody: Hendrickson, 1994), 3.1, 9:62.

that his love for us is just a quid pro quo relationship. We scratch his back so he scratches ours. The Bible magnifies the wonder of God's love by testifying to his self-sufficiency. For no gain or benefit, he has poured out his love upon us.

Prayer

'Heavenly Father, forgive me for the times when I have thought I could place you in my debt because of what I give you. Forgive me for the times when I have thought myself necessary to the work of your kingdom. Grant me a right humility and an awareness that I add nothing to your life.

'I acknowledge that you do not depend on any of the things you have made. You are not an idol that hungers or thirsts and needs people to bring it food and drink. You do not need any creature. You do not need me. You are independent of all you have made, sufficient for yourself, the great I AM. You are independent of me. You are not made strong by human sacrifices. You are not made strong by my sacrifices.

'I praise you that you have made such a rich creation, filled with diversity to reflect the richness of your life, imaging you not to add to your ever-perfect life, but to reflect that life to us.

'I marvel that you love your people without needing us. Fill me with delight as I think of how you love me without any necessity. I praise you for your uncaused, self-caused love. In Christ's name. Amen.'

7. LOVE THAT IS ALWAYS IN CONTROL

Helplessly in love

An amusing book by Max Beerbohm tells the tale of Zuleika Dobson, a young woman, a literal femme fatale, coming to Oxford where her grandfather is the Warden of Judas College. The whole of Oxford falls in love with her, but their affection remains unrequited because she will love only a man who can resist her charms. From the moment she sets foot off the train, she leaves men broken-hearted in her wake. Her greatest victim is the Duke of Dorset. An ancient tradition states that on the eve of a Duke's death two black owls will perch on the battlements of the family estate, Tankerton Hall. At one point in the story the Duke is in Oxford and receives a telegram from his butler:

Deeply regret inform your grace last night two black owls came and perched on battlements remained there through night hooting at dawn flew away none knows whither awaiting instructions

Jellings

The Duke promptly replies:

Jellings Tankerton Hall
Prepare vault for funeral Monday

$$\textit{Dorset}^1$$

Later that day the Duke drowns himself in the Isis (Oxford's name for the river Thames). Then all of his fellow undergraduates, except for one, do the same. The last survivor does not last long, jumping in shame from a window in the midst of a commotion. Zuleika, Beerbohm writes, 'had taken full toll now'.[2] The novel ends with her ordering a special train to take her to . . . Cambridge!

Beerbohm's novel is a witty tale about the captivating power of a woman over love-sick undergraduates. It is a comedy we must not take too seriously (let the romantically inclined take note!). Nonetheless, amid the amusement the novel reveals in exaggerated form something of how we often think about love, something we have already seen in the tragically true story of Abelard and Heloise: romantic love usually happens *to* us. It arises within us when it is evoked by an object outside ourselves. The undergraduates who fell for Zuleika could not help themselves: they were helplessly in love.

Many are familiar with this feeling, perhaps especially in the first flush of romantic love in a new relationship. Your loved one fills your thoughts. You cannot get her out of your mind. She has captured your heart. You constantly wonder if your love will be reciprocated. You are nervous when you see her, stumbling over your words like a bumbling fool. Like a Roman haruspex poring over the entrails of a dead bird, you interpret every sign of what she might think about you. Does she feel for me what I feel for her? Should I declare my interest now, or is it too soon?

God is not like the Duke of Dorset: he is not helplessly in love with his people. One of the most striking differences in divine love is that it is sovereignly willed by God. It is not his response to an object that captivates him. He does not 'fall for' his creation.

---

1. Max Beerbohm, *Zuleika Dobson* (London: Minerva, 1991), p. 156.
2. Ibid., p. 236.

I do not mean that God is devoid of affection for his people, that he feels nothing for them. Nor do I mean that he does not find them beautiful. My point is that when he feels affection and when he finds them beautiful, this is by his own sovereign will, not because they have drawn such a love from him.

Sovereign love creates and sustains

We know that God loves sovereignly because he creates and sustains the objects of his love. He is utterly in control of them because they owe every moment of their existence to him. The triune God brings creatures into being out of nothing. In John's vision of heaven he sees the elders praising God as creator:

> Worthy are you, our Lord and God,
>   to receive glory and honour and power,
> for you created all things,
>   and by your will they existed and were created.
> (Rev. 4:11)

John writes of the Word who became flesh that 'without him was not any thing made that was made' (John 1:3), and in Genesis we read of the Spirit of God 'hovering over the face of the waters' (1:2).

Having made us, the triune God keeps us in existence. We depend on him constantly for our very being, as Paul tells the Athenians when he quotes from one of the Greek poets: 'In him we live and move and have our being' (Acts 17:28). We are sustained by Christ in whom 'all things hold together' (Col. 1:17). God's love is sovereign love because he creates and sustains the existence of his beloved.

God does not come across his creatures like someone finding a new friend. He does not create them and leave them to grow and then later on discover that he loves what they have become in their independent existence. None of the objects of God's love ever has an existence independent from him. All creatures continue to depend on God for every moment of their existence. Even as he loves them, they owe their existence to him. God wills what he loves, and he wills to love it. In his love he goes entirely before his creatures.

He decrees in eternity and then effects in time our existence and persistence.

Sovereign love chooses and draws

A second reason for thinking that God loves sovereignly is that when he draws people to himself, he does so of his own good pleasure. He does not choose people because he foreknows that they will say 'Yes' to him. If he did, there would be no one to choose, because left to ourselves we are all weak and helpless, slaves to sin and dead in it (John 8:34; Eph. 2:1). Just as dead people do not raise themselves, so we would never take the initiative in responding to God. Rather, God effectually changes the hearts of his chosen people so that they are irresistibly drawn to him and kept by him to the end (John 6:44). In one of his prayers the apostle Paul explains that God purposes his electing love from before the creation of the world according to his own will:

> Blessed be the God and Father of our Lord Jesus Christ, who has blessed us in Christ with every spiritual blessing in the heavenly places, even as he chose us in him before the foundation of the world, that we should be holy and blameless before him. In love he predestined us for adoption as sons through Jesus Christ, according to the purpose of his will, to the praise of his glorious grace, with which he has blessed us in the Beloved. (Eph. 1:3–6)

When God chose his people before the creation of the world, he did not look into the future, see what they would be like, fall in love with and then choose them, as if he were always playing catch-up with his people's choices. Paul's prayer shows that God eternally wills the choices of his people. He does not just foresee them and then conform his will to their will. He chooses us by his own will: 'In him we have obtained an inheritance, having been predestined according to the purpose of him who works all things according to the counsel of his will' (Eph. 1:11).

While Paul here focuses his praise on the Father, this sovereign election is the work of the triune God. Jesus himself explains that the Father's choice is also the Son's choice: 'no one knows the Father except the Son and anyone to whom the Son chooses to reveal him' (Matt. 11:27). This is why Jesus can say to his disciples, 'You did not choose me, but I chose you' (John 15:16). And he teaches that the Spirit chooses as he wills: 'The wind blows where it wishes, and you hear its sound, but you do not know where it comes from or where it goes. So it is with everyone who is born of the Spirit' (John 3:8).

This does not mean that we are inactive in our salvation, or that we cannot be commanded to repent, believe and persevere. Think of the disciples to whom Jesus said in John 15 that he had chosen them: they had listened to his call, left their boats and followed him. We read of their seeking (1:38), coming (1:39, 46) and finding (1:40, 45). The sovereignty of God does not annihilate the human will and human action, but it does explain them. We are not to think that we make no choices, but that when we make choices we do so moved irresistibly by the Spirit of God. We follow Jesus because the Father draws us to the Son, because the Son reveals the Father to us and because the Spirit gives us new birth.

The Spirit is not like a kidnapper carrying a man away with his hands and feet bound, the man screaming in protest at every step. Yet in the moment that he gives the miracle of new birth the Spirit acts against all the previous inclinations of our fallen nature. In that act of resurrection we are indeed passive. By nature we are spiritually dead in trespasses and sins (Eph. 2:1). A dead person cannot raise himself. No one can come unless drawn. In the moment of regeneration, the moment when God 'made us alive together with Christ' (Eph. 2:5), our souls are made new creations in Christ Jesus (Eph. 2:10), alive to God in him. By the Spirit who blows where he wills, God gives us a new heart and a new spirit (Ezek. 36:26). The moment of regeneration is an act in which we are utterly passive as life is breathed into our dead souls. Were it not so, we could not be saved. As John Murray writes:

> If it were not the case that in regeneration we are passive, the subjects
> of an action of which God alone is the agent, there would be no gospel
> at all. For unless God by sovereign, operative grace had turned our

enmity to love and our disbelief to faith we would never yield the
response of faith and love.[3]

Being regenerated by a sovereign, instantaneous, recreative act
of the Spirit, the person repents and trusts in Christ. In those
acts of conversion the new human heart is active. The new believer
depends entirely on the work of the Spirit in regeneration, but
following that miracle in which he is passive he is subsequently
spiritually active. He does not act by himself. He does not cooperate
from a position of spiritual neutrality, making his own mind up, but
he is active. His repentance and faith continue to be dependent on
the sovereign work of the Spirit, but he does repent and believe.
Repentance, faith and Christian living are not a zero-sum game in
which it is either God who acts or the believer. The exercise of
repentance and faith is entirely worked by the Spirit, and is the work
of the believer.

In the moment of regeneration, the moment that the spiritually
dead body is brought to life in the tomb of sin, the person is inactive.
As he repents and believes, as he rises and walks for the first time,
he is still wholly dependent, but is now active. The Holy Spirit works
not by abolishing the human mind and will but by renewing them,
so that the believer himself believes. He does not leave us in death
while forcing us to do what he wants: he breathes new life into us.
Christ comes to us as a sovereign yet gentle Lord, whose regenerating Spirit enables us to respond both to his command to repent
and believe, and to his gentle invitation to find rest in him.

We do not make the difference

The main historical alternative to this teaching on divine sovereignty
is that God chooses those he foreknows will choose him. His
choice is responsive to our choice. On this classical Arminian view,
God is not truly sovereign in the drawing of a sinner. His love is

---

3. John Murray, *Redemption Accomplished and Applied* (Edinburgh: Banner
   of Truth Trust, 1961), p. 100.

more like the love of a human lover, responsive to what it finds in the beloved. I do not mean to suggest that it is totally the same as human love. That would be to misrepresent the Arminian view. A theologian such as John Wesley, for example, is quite clear that God still acts first in salvation and that we could never turn to him without his first turning towards us. Wesley teaches that we are by nature dead in sin. The Father sends the Son, and he works by his Spirit to restore fallen sinners to the point where they can respond freely to the gospel. This restoration occurs through his 'prevenient grace'. But having restored the capacity, God then lets his creatures determine their own response, on the basis of which he chooses any who choose him.

The problem with this understanding of God's action is that it surrenders control of the defining and distinguishing moments in our salvation to us. In a free-will theology like classical Arminianism Christ accomplishes his saving work for everyone and offers the same salvation to everyone. The goodness of God is understood to require this common treatment. But if we then ask why on this view some are saved and some lost, the distinguishing difference is found in our own varying human responses. Some of us have made the right choice with our free will, and some have made the wrong choice. The distinction between a Christian and a non-Christian, the difference that saves one and condemns the other, is attributed to their own restored will making its undetermined choices. In most free-will theologies this explanation extends beyond the initial response of faith in conversion to every successive decision to persevere with the Lord. Free will is exercised all the way to the deathbed.

Attributing our salvation to our own free will in this way is theologically wrong and spiritually disastrous. The response may come that in Arminian theology our salvation is not 'attributed' to us. But the fact that *the* act that distinguishes the saved from the lost is explained as a choice made with libertarian freedom reveals that at just the point which matters *we* are the cause of our salvation. God does the same for everyone. The distinguishing feature of those saved is that they themselves made the right decision and kept making it. Their initial choice and perseverance is the only thing that distinguishes them from the lost, and *they* did it.

Happily, Christians who advocate this kind of theology do not in my experience follow the spiritual logic of their theological position. If they did, then they would have to praise themselves for their choice in all of those crucial moments that distinguish them from the lost. But because they are regenerate people, born again by the very sovereign grace they deny, they praise God for his gift of salvation. The logical outworking of the Arminian system contrasts with the praise of Paul, but the spirituality of most Arminians I know does not. Despite their theology they pray with Paul, 'Blessed be the God and Father of our Lord Jesus Christ . . .' (Eph. 1:3). Arminians are rescued by their inconsistency. Indeed, so are all Christians. Not one of us holds a perfect theology. Any single error we hold could, if pushed to its logical consequences, destroy our whole system. It is only our inconsistency that prevents it doing so. God uses even our illogicality to protect us!

The strong man

A third reason for thinking that God's love is sovereign is the way Scripture describes salvation as a work of conquest. The messianic hope that runs throughout the Bible focuses on a figure who will conquer Satan, set humanity free and bring them under the rule of God. Immediately after the fall God promises that one of the offspring of Eve will be the serpent crusher (Gen. 3:15). As the Old Testament history unfolds, many figures typify the coming Christ by conquering the enemies of God's people. Abraham wages war against the Canaanite kings; Moses leads the people out of bondage to Pharaoh; Joshua triumphs over the wicked inhabitants of the Promised Land; judges such as Gideon and Samson fight against Midianites and Philistines; Saul and David carry on that unfinished battle; and Solomon brings the Promised Land to its greatest extent.

When the Christ comes and is accused by the scribes of casting out demons by the power of Beelzebub the prince of demons, he asks:

> if Satan has risen up against himself and is divided, he cannot stand,
> but is coming to an end. But no one can enter a strong man's house and

plunder his goods, unless he first binds the strong man. Then indeed he may plunder his house. (Mark 3:26–27)

Here Jesus argues that, far from being on the side of Beelzebub, he is the one who has come to tie him up in order to plunder him, to take back from him what he has stolen.

This talk of conquest does not mean that Christ's victory is achieved by outward military means. Far from it. Jesus entered the house of the strong man and bound him by entering the house of death and himself being struck on the heel. He turned away from political or military power and towards Calvary. When the crowds tried to make him king, he withdrew from them (John 6:15). When Peter cut off Malchus' ear, Jesus healed the wound and told Peter to sheath his sword. He came not to fight but to suffer (Luke 22:51; John 18:10–11). It was precisely by means of his seemingly weak and powerless suffering that Jesus accomplished his great victory. It was by dying that he 'disarmed the rulers and authorities and put them to open shame' (Col. 2:15). Christ was victor not despite his death, but in his death. He cancelled the legal debt we owed by paying, on our behalf, the price for our sins (Col. 2:14; 1 Peter 1:18–19). By bearing the punishment of sin in our place he destroyed the one who wielded the power of death (Isa. 53:4–6, 10–12; Heb. 2:14–15). By his resurrection he drew the sting of death when he died under the curse of the law (Gal. 3:13; 1 Cor. 15:56–57).

Now ascended to the right hand of God, Christ rules over the church while his enemies are brought into submission under his feet (Heb. 1:13). The cross was his path to exaltation: having given himself for the church (Eph. 5:25), Christ came to reign over all things for her (Eph. 1:19–22). When he returns, he will come as King of kings and Lord of lords to conquer finally all of his enemies by the sword that comes from his mouth (Rev. 19:11–21). The whole story of the Bible from the beginning to the end is the story of God's Messiah coming as king to conquer his enemies and rescue his people.

Meditation

God's love is different from our love because he is always sovereign in his love. He is sovereign because unlike us he creates, sustains and draws the people he loves. His love is vividly depicted throughout Scripture as the love of a conquering king, though a king unlike any other in that he conquers through the weakness of the cross. Here is a great mystery. Jesus' moment of greatest weakness was actually his moment of greatest power. When he appeared to have lost, he was winning the decisive victory. There is, therefore, something of extraordinary tenderness in the kingship of Jesus, because his strength was exercised not by terrifying muscular might, but by laying down his life in agony. Jesus exercises an unstoppable power, but does so through being crucified, not through the application of violent force.

- *Read John's passion narrative (John 18 – 19). How do you see the sovereignty of Jesus in the midst of his suffering?*

We also see the mighty tenderness of God in the regeneration and conversion of the believer. The Holy Spirit mercifully brings the dead to new life. He works a miracle on those who cannot help themselves. But then he does not drag his new creature along the pavements of the Christian life, like some disobedient dog constantly straining against its master's leash. Rather, he so changes the heart of his indwelt people that they will to repent, to believe and to live for Christ. Obviously his work of recreation is in one sense not yet complete: the sinful nature remains at war with the Spirit, and the body remains perishable. But we are definitively new creatures, and our true selves walk with the Spirit even though the remnant of the old self resists.

- *Think back over the work of the Spirit in your life and return thanks to God for it.*

The sovereign, gentle love of God in salvation is at once humbling and encouraging. It is humbling because it reminds us that we owe the entirety of our salvation to God. Even when our regenerated hearts will to repent and believe, they do so in entire dependence on God. There is no freedom of indifference for us, no moment in which we make an uninfluenced choice to believe. There is no shuttered-off realm of free choice in which we, prompted only from the outside by the Spirit, decide what we want to do. If God's work were resistible, that is what we would be saying: we would be maintaining some act of the soul in which we could choose to resist the work of the Spirit. There would be such a space somewhere in us, protected against the work of the Spirit to such an extent that we could make our own minds up. But there is no private office for us, the CEO of our soul, from the door of which the Spirit of God can only plead for us to respond. Our entire person with every faculty involved in decision-making is open-plan to the pervasive work of the Spirit. There is no moment of our response to God that the Spirit does not penetrate and carry along.

This is humbling, because we see that we are not the neutral arbiters of truth we think we are. We are simply guilty rebels against God and helpless victims of the devil, lying dead in the tomb. The Spirit is the one who works the initial miracle of regeneration and then irresistibly sustains every moment of our new life.

Such a vision of the sovereignty of God's love is often offensive, even to Christian ears, as it may be to yours. Often the way in which we first heard the gospel encouraged us to think that we are indeed the sovereign arbiters of truth. God was invited to bring in his arguments for us to weigh. He was called to plead his evidence in the court where we sat as judge. Millions have been genuinely converted through such man-exalting apologetics, but many of them have then struggled to accept that they are not who they thought they were, and even who the evangelist implied they were.

I speak from personal experience: for a considerable time after my conversion I resisted vehemently the idea of God's sovereignty in salvation. In the end, confronted by texts such as Romans 9 and Ephesians 1, I capitulated, but I did so reluctantly and with little joy. It was my awareness of my own sin that finally convinced me that I should rejoice in the idea of irresistible grace. I grasped that my sinfulness ran so deep that I would certainly have resisted any grace that could be resisted. There was no possibility that I could have made the right response to the gospel without being irresistibly drawn. Apart from the all-pervading grace of God, I would never have believed.

- *Does your theology seek to preserve for yourself a corner of salvation over which you make a choice that is not wholly explained by the sovereign work of the Spirit?*

- *Do you think you have the capacity to respond rightly to a resistible work of the Holy Spirit?*

The sovereignty of God's love in salvation is encouraging for the same reason that it is humbling: it reminds us that we cannot save ourselves, and that our perseverance in the Christian life does not depend on us. If there were a private office where I, the CEO of my soul, had to make a choice to believe influenced only by the *resistible* work of the Spirit, then I would need constantly to be worried that as I sit alone in that office I might make the wrong response. If no such space exists and all of the work of God in me has been sovereign so far, then I can trust that it will continue to be so into the future. My final perseverance, while it is something in which I am active, does not depend on my making again and again the right decision to respond to the grace of God that is at every turn resistible. Paul tells the Philippians that he is sure 'that he who began a good work in you will bring it to completion at the day of Jesus Christ' (1:6). Later in the same letter he tells them, 'work out your own salvation with fear and trembling', but immediately adds the basis of that command in God's sovereignty: 'for it is God who works in you, both to will and to work for his good pleasure' (Phil. 2:12–13). What God has begun he will finish.

- *Consciously set aside the idea that your perseverance rests on you alone.*

- *Dwell on the fact that God completes the work he begins.*

Prayer

'Heavenly Father, I praise you for your sovereign love that purposes, creates and sustains all things. You created me. You knitted me together in my mother's womb. You sustain me from breath to breath. Every moment my existence is upheld only by you. You have numbered my days from before the creation of the world.

'You are utterly sovereign in my salvation. Your kingly Son came in power to save, yet he came in humility, stooping lower than any man has ever stooped, even to death on the cross.

'Your Holy Spirit has changed my heart and made it new. I acknowledge that every response I have made to you has been worked in me by your sovereign Spirit. Humble me before you, I pray, and encourage me with the truth of my utter dependence on you.

'Thank you for the great promise that you will finish in me what you have begun. Help me moment by moment to work out my salvation with fear and trembling, confident that it is you at work in me.

'I praise you for your sovereign love, that there is nothing I have that I did not receive. In Christ's mighty name. Amen.'

8. TIMELESS LOVE THAT NEVER CHANGES

Romeo and . . . Rosaline?

Shakespeare's tragedy *Romeo and Juliet* is rightly known for its depiction of the 'star-cross'd lovers' and their 'death-mark'd love', but we may forget that the play begins with Romeo completely devoted to another Capulet, Rosaline.[1] Soon after the opening of the play Lady Montague, Romeo's mother, is looking for her son. His friend Benvolio tells her that he saw him early in the morning sitting unhappily under a grove of sycamore trees. Lady Montague comments that her son has often been seen there, 'With tears augmenting the fresh morning's dew, / Adding to clouds more clouds with his deep sighs.'[2]

At this point Romeo himself enters and his mother departs. The cause of his melancholy is now revealed: his love for Rosaline is

---

1. William Shakespeare, *Romeo and Juliet*, ed. René Weis (London: Bloomsbury, 2012; repr. 2013), Prologue, ll. 6, 9, pp. 123, 124.
2. Ibid. I. i. 130–131, p. 133.

unrequited. Romeo describes his condition in strong terms. He lives
in a kind of death because of Rosaline:

> She hath forsworn to love, and in that vow
> Do I live dead that live to tell it now.[3]

He feels like a man locked in prison, kept without food, whipped and
tormented.[4] Benvolio urges Romeo to 'Examine other beauties'.[5] But
Romeo insists that this will only make matters worse:

> Show me a mistress that is passing fair,
> What doth her beauty serve but as a note
> Where I may read who passed that passing fair?[6]

Romeo seems utterly convinced that Rosaline is the only lady he can
love. When they hear about the Capulet feast being held that evening,
Benvolio urges Romeo to go so that he can compare her to other
women, confident that he will come to think his 'swan a crow'.[7] Romeo
disavows any such possibility as a kind of heresy deserving death:

> When the devout religion of mine eye
> Maintains such falsehood, then turn tears to fire,
> And these who, often drowned, could never die,
> Transparent heretics, be burnt for liars.
> One fairer than my love! The all-seeing sun
> Ne'er saw her match since first the world begun.[8]

All the evidence suggests that Romeo has sworn undying love for
Rosaline, and that he has consigned himself to a prison of melancholy without her.

---

3. Ibid. 221–222, p. 140.
4. Ibid. ii. 53–54.
5. Ibid. i. 226, p. 141.
6. Ibid. 232–234, p. 141.
7. Ibid. ii. 88, p. 147.
8. Ibid. 89–94, p. 147.

How sudden is the transfer of his affection when, at the Capulet feast, he sets eyes on Juliet! All his love for Rosaline evaporates:

> Did my heart love till now? Forswear it, sight,
> For I ne'er saw true beauty till this night.[9]

So fast is the change that it takes some time for his friends to catch up. When in the next scene Mercutio cannot find Romeo, he tries to conjure him up by appealing to 'Rosaline's bright eyes' and other parts of her body.[10] Juliet also comes to love Romeo suddenly, and is worried about his response to such suddenness:

> Or if thou think'st I am too quickly won,
> I'll frown and be perverse and say thee nay.[11]

She fears that they are making their vows of love too soon:

> I have no joy of this contract tonight;
> It is too rash, too unadvised, too sudden,
> Too like the lightning which doth cease to be
> Ere one can say 'it lightens'.[12]

When Romeo asks Friar Laurence to marry them, the friar is amazed by the sudden departure of his affections from Rosaline:

> Holy Saint Francis, what a change is here!
> Is Rosaline, that thou didst love so dear,
> So soon forsaken?[13]

Shakespeare may even indicate that Romeo has simply found in Juliet a Rosaline substitute, transferring his love from one rose to

---

9. Ibid. v. 51–52, p. 170.
10. Ibid. II. i. 17–21, p. 182.
11. Ibid. ii. 95–96, p. 192.
12. Ibid. 117–120, p. 194.
13. Ibid. iii. 61–63, p. 205.

another. When Juliet comments that 'That which we call a rose / By any other word would smell as sweet', she is speaking about Romeo's name.[14] But in Shakespeare's time 'Rosaline' was thought to mean 'lovely rose' (from Rosalind, *rosa linda*), so some critics have suggested that Romeo's idealized rose changes easily from Rosaline to Juliet.[15] Love moves on.

It is a little ironic that a story that ends with Romeo and Juliet paying the ultimate price for their love begins with Romeo so casually leaving behind his devotion to Rosaline. Ironic perhaps, but human love is often like this. A relationship felt to be utterly unique and totally irreplaceable soon gives way to another. At least Romeo's love did find a resting place, whereas all too often human love keeps moving on, from a Rosaline to a Juliet to an Ophelia to a Desdemona. A man finds The One, then he finds the next The One and the next The One (belying the definite article, the substantive and the capitals!). A woman has so many boyfriends in such quick succession that her friends cannot keep track of their names. In our own times even husbands and wives come and go with alacrity. We know, often with shameful and painful clarity, that human love can be short lived and changeable.

The creator God's love is eternal

God's love is different from human love because it is eternal and, therefore, unchanging. His love is unaltered by the passage of time because God exists beyond time. Because God is eternal, we can be confident he will never move on in his affections.

While the Bible does not contain detailed reflections on how God relates to time, it does teach that he is its creator, and thus lies beyond it. In Genesis we read that God created the markers used to measure time, the lights in the heavens 'for signs and for seasons, and for days and years' (Gen. 1:14). But we also read that he created the

---

14. Ibid. ii. 43–44, p. 189.

15. Patrick Hanks, Kate Hardcastle and Flavia Hodges, *A Dictionary of First Names*, 2nd ed. (Oxford: Oxford University Press, 2006), p. 234.

heavens and the earth and the days themselves, indicating that he made the whole of space and time. The biblical teaching that to the Lord one day is like a thousand years and a thousand years are like a day (2 Peter 3:8) shows that he is not bound to the passage of time as we are.

This biblical argument coheres with the insight of modern physics that space and time exist together, as explained by Albert Einstein. If God created all spatial reality, then science suggests he created all temporal reality too. As the creator of space and time, God is outside and beyond them. He is present to all times and spaces, but is contained by none.

The triune God's love is eternal

The doctrine of creation shows that God's love is timeless love, and so does the doctrine of the Trinity. There remains more work to be done by theologians on integrating our understanding of his attributes, such as his eternality, with our understanding of his triune life. What difference to our understanding of God's attributes does the Trinity make? We have too often separated our discussion of the oneness of God from our discussion of the three persons, as if the threeness of God makes no difference to the divine attributes the persons share. My point is not that it is always wrong to have separate chapters in a systematic theology on 'God as Trinity' and 'God is love'. Chapter divisions have to come somewhere, so a formal separation of closely related elements cannot be avoided. The problem arises when there is an actual separation of the content as well, leaving the triunity of God unrelated to his attributes.

Theologians have been at their best in avoiding this kind of separation when they have discussed the divine attribute of love. They have rightly described the love of God in trinitarian terms, explaining that God is love because of the mutual love of the persons of the Godhead. I have not seen the same degree of attention to the triune life of God in the description of his other attributes such as eternality. If we do not make these links, the risk is that we give an account of the divine attributes that would do just as well for any monotheist system, such as Islam, as it does for the one true God.

Far from being unrelated, the doctrine of the Trinity actually requires a doctrine of divine eternality. The persons of the Holy Trinity indwell one another. The Father is in the Son and the Son is in the Father (John 14:11). As the names 'Father' and 'Son' show, the Father indwells the Son as the one who begets him, and the Son indwells the Father because his being is from the Father. In other words, it is as the Son, the only-begotten Son, that the Son is in the Father. The Son is *in* the Father because he is *from* the Father. This is why the Son can make the Father known: because he fully indwells the Father and is indwelt by him. This mutual indwelling of the persons cannot change or increase. Paul tells us that God indwells Christ fully: 'in him all the fullness of God was pleased to dwell' (Col. 1:19). The Father does not hold back from the Son.

Here we come to the link to eternality. Imagine that the triune God is in time, that he lives his divine life through the course of time. This would mean that the Son is begotten by the Father in time. If the Son is begotten in time, then the begetting must have a beginning. If the begetting had a beginning, then there was a time when the Son was not. This is the Arian heresy, a denial of the doctrine of the Trinity, because the Son would then be a creature. Someone might say that the Son need not have a beginning: he could simply have always been being begotten. But even then he would have much of his begotten life ahead of him, still to come. Indeed, given that he will last for ever through time, he would have an infinite future of his begotten life as yet unrealized at any point in time. Similarly, the Father would always have an infinite future of begetting still to come. The triune life of the Father and the Son would then be for ever incomplete; there would be more begetting to come for the Father and more begottenness to come for the Son. This would also be a denial of the orthodox doctrine of the Trinity.

If, however, the Father begets the Son in eternity, outside time, then the act has no beginning, no end, and is eternally complete. There is no possibility of incompleteness. Hilary of Poitiers explains this in his classic work *On the Trinity*. He insists that even though we struggle to imagine what an eternal birth is, we can see that only an eternal birth does not have a beginning: 'He Who was born before times eternal, has always been born, although we can form no positive conception of anything having been born before all time.'[16] With its insistence on the fullness of the triune relations, the orthodox doctrine of the Trinity requires that God and his love be eternal.

God is changeless in being and act

The timelessness of God means that, unlike us, he neither leaves behind nor waits for any of his life. He does not lose his yesterday, and he does not gain his tomorrow. He simply is. To say that God is timeless in his love, therefore, implies that he is also changeless. As James puts it in his epistle, with God 'there is no variation or shadow due to change' (1:17). To use the technical term, God is 'immutable'.

Given that he is immutable in his being, God is also constant in his dealings with his creation: how God acts reflects who he is. Because God does not change in his being, he does not change in his purposes. He makes covenants he will certainly keep. The connection moves both ways: from God's inner life to his outward acts, and from his outward acts to his inner life. In terms of the order of being, the order of reality itself, his inner life comes first and his outward acts are derived from it. The constancy of his acts rests on the constancy of his being. In terms of the order of our knowing, his outward acts come first, since it is from them that we understand his inner life. God shows himself to us as he really is. The constancy of his acts reveals the constancy of his being. Being good and true, he does not show himself to be one way while secretly being another. He does not deceive us about who he is. His inner immutability grounds his covenant faithfulness.

---

16. Hilary of Poitiers, *On the Trinity*, in Philip Schaff and Henry Wace
    (eds.), *Nicene and Post-Nicene Fathers*, second series, 14 vols. (Buffalo:
    Christian Literature, 1886–90; repr. Peabody: Hendrickson, 1994),
    12.28, 9:225.

One of the clearest passages showing God's unchanging plans is in the book of Numbers. Balak the king of Moab tries to recruit Balaam son of Beor to put a curse on the Israelites. God refuses to let Balaam curse the Israelites and obstructs his attempts. One of Balaam's oracles explains that the Israelites cannot be cursed because God has purposed to bless them:

> God is not man, that he should lie,
>> or a son of man, that he should change his mind.
> Has he said, and will he not do it?
>> Or has he spoken, and will he not fulfil it?
> (Num. 23:19)

The implications of these words extend far beyond this one incident. The oracle explains that God does not change his mind, because he is not a man. The argument is simple enough: men change their minds; God, not being a man, does not change his mind. If we claim that God changes his plans, then we might as well say that he ceases to be God. To posit change in God is to un-God him, to turn him into a man.

The Trinity means God is changeless in being

As with eternity, we should try to see how the attribute of immutability relates to the triune life of God. First, we consider the changelessness of the loving being of God. Is there a particular link between the Trinity and God's not changing in his being? Part of the answer must be that the changelessness of God lies in the changelessness of the relationships between the divine persons. It is because of the constancy of the relationships between the persons that God does not change. The relationships are constant because they are perfect in love. The Father does not need his relationship with the Son to break new ground: there is no new ground for it to break because it is for ever maximally realized, leaving nothing to be changed that might deepen it. Nor could anything ever be lost from it to make it less than it already is. The perfection of the loving triune relationships means that God does not change in his being.

The Trinity means God is changeless in purpose

The triune God is also unchanging in his loving purpose. Here we must recall that in eternity the Father lays the work of salvation upon the Son and the Son undertakes to accomplish it. As Jesus puts it, 'I have come down from heaven, not to do my own will but the will of him who sent me' (John 6:38). Evidently this will was proposed to him in heaven before he came down, and he came to do it. The writer to the Hebrews describes Jesus' speaking the words of Psalm 40 at his incarnation: 'Behold, I have come to do your will, O God' (Heb. 10:7). Jesus came from heaven with a purpose. When the Son accomplishes the work he was sent to do, the Father delights to give him his reward of glory:

> being found in human form, he humbled himself by becoming obedient to the point of death, even death on a cross. Therefore God has highly exalted him and bestowed on him the name that is above every name, so that at the name of Jesus every knee should bow, in heaven and on earth and under the earth, and every tongue confess that Jesus Christ is Lord, to the glory of God the Father. (Phil. 2:8–11)

Note the 'therefore': the exaltation of Jesus is the result of his obedience in death.

Reformed theologians have called this plan of salvation proposed by the Father and undertaken by the Son the 'covenant of redemption'. In this covenant we see how the Trinity grounds the unchangeable purposes of God. The plan of salvation begins in the single will of the triune God willed by each of the persons in eternity. It finds its stability in the promise made by the Father to the Son and the Son to the Father. Any change in the purposes of God would mean breaking the covenant made between the divine persons. Since the divine persons relate to each other with perfect faithfulness, such a break is unthinkable. The fact that God is the triune God who covenants within himself for our redemption means that his purposes can never change. God's covenanted plan had our salvation fixed in place before the world began.

The covenant between the persons of the Trinity is good news for sinners because it means our redemption was put in place in eternity, as Patrick Gillespie explains:

> How should that support faith, and comfort and assure our hearts, that the love of God and of Christ did provide a rich inheritance for us when we were not yet created, and did provide a physician before we fell sick: who had a Redeemer in readiness, before the fall of Man, which he foresaw: who provided a Surety before he was needed, to be in readiness to strike hands for our Debt; that Christ spoke kindly for us, when we were not present: that he took our case in hand undesired: that he undertook for us when we had neither being, nor action, nor vote, nor knowledge of his undertaking.[17]

God speaks of creaturely change

Having said all of this, in his loving interaction with us in time, God speaks of himself changing. Most notably perhaps, he changes his mind about destroying the Israelites for worshipping the golden calf when Moses intercedes for them: 'And the LORD relented from the disaster that he had spoken of bringing on his people' (Exod. 32:14). How are we to explain this when other passages state that he is changeless?

We already have an answer implicit within the framework for understanding revelation that I set out in chapter 2. We saw there that when God reveals himself to us, he does so in thoroughly creaturely terms. He speaks analogically, using the things he has made to describe himself so that we can know him. He says all sorts of things about himself that, read in artificial isolation, could be misunderstood. For example, we might conclude from the statement 'our God is a consuming fire' (Heb. 12:29) that, like the Zoroastrians, we should all worship fire. But reading the Bible properly, allowing it to interpret itself, prevents us reaching such conclusions. The rest of Scripture shows us that God is spirit, and that the description of

---

17. Patrick Gillespie, *The Ark of the Covenant Opened: Or, A Treatise of the Covenant of Redemption* (London: Thomas Parkhurst, 1677), p. 129.

him as fire is intended to teach us to worship him with reverence because he punishes sinners.

So too with God's changing. God speaks of himself as changing to show that his loving relationship with us is real, that he does interact with us, that our prayers are effective. In his secret counsel he had eternally willed to 'change' in response to Moses, so that the change was no actual change in God himself or his plan, but he had also willed to interact in a human-like way with Moses. He had decreed the prayer of Moses and his response. This is why he speaks of himself as changing.

Is this deceptive? Does God appear to be one way when in fact he is another? It is not, because the wider scope of God's revelation makes clear that creaturely language has its limits, and that we need to read all of Scripture together in an integrated fashion to understand the parts of it correctly. It is no more deceptive for God to speak of himself changing than it is for Jesus to call himself the good shepherd: in both cases the context, wider or narrower, makes clear the way in which the description should be understood, and prevents us applying it to God in all its details.

The priority of biblical language

Having said that God does not change in himself even though he uses the language of change, it is very important to state that God knows best how to describe himself. As I argued in chapter 2, the way God reveals himself in creaturely terms is the way he always intended to reveal himself. It is Plan A, not Plan B. We must never think that there is something wrong with the Bible when it describes God's changing. Human systematic theological language is not more hygienic than biblical language, as if the Bible speaks a language unfortunately dirtied by time and change while systematic theology has cleansed itself of such impurities. God authored the Bible, so there is nothing unfortunate about the way he describes himself in it. If I find myself thinking, 'I wish he hadn't put it like that,' I am going astray.

And of course systematic theology itself, like all human discourse, is conducted in creaturely language. For example, it may get us closer to describing God's existence in literal terms when it points out that God is beyond time, but it too ends up using time-bound language of God. Even the most famous definition of eternity from the Christian philosopher Boethius does so: he wrote that eternity is 'the whole, simultaneous and perfect possession of boundless life'.[18] 'Simultaneous' is a temporal term.

There must be no great division between systematic and biblical theology. When systematic theology points out that God's life is not literally lived in the present tense, it does so on the basis of the biblical doctrine that God created time. Scripture itself shows us that its application of the present tense to the life of God – for example, when Jesus says, 'before Abraham was, I am' (John 8:58) – is analogical, because it teaches us that God is the creator of time. This is not some extra-biblical insight or a conclusion of systematic theology operating in superior isolation. God himself shows us in his Word that his love is different from human love because it is eternal and unchanging.

Meditation

We live in an age of unfaithfulness. No doubt all the ages of man east of Eden have been ages of unfaithfulness. The fall did not happen with the death of Queen Victoria or the coming of 1960. Nevertheless, our own era has made its unfaithfulness more apparent, a point made by the evidence I discussed in chapter 5 for rising levels of divorce and fatherlessness. All but the most hardened person must know how tragic family breakdown is. Despite the bravado and the rhetoric of 'new beginnings', I am confident that no one who has drawn close to another person in marriage and then experienced that bond being broken actually thinks lightly of it. No one whose action has broken a home around the life of a small child can really believe that a new set of plural families can be constructed

---

18. Boethius, *The Consolation of Philosophy*, tr. S. J. Tester, in *Boethius*, Loeb Classical Library 74 (Cambridge, Mass.: Harvard University Press; London: William Heinemann, 1973; repr. 1978), 5.6, p. 423.

for the child with no harmful effect. It is simply a self-justifying trick to tell a child divided between two homes and two new pairs of partners that the arrangement is somehow to its advantage, as if two 'mothers' or 'fathers' were better than one.

The immutability and covenant faithfulness of God is good news for sinners whose lives are surrounded and pervaded by the unfaithfulness of which family breakdown is simply the most obvious symptom. We may experience broken trust in so many ways: with our spouses, with our in-laws and extended families, with our friends, with our employers, even with our pastors. In-laws may fail to let their sons leave and cleave to their wives. Friends may turn against one another. Employers may fail to meet their obligations and take unjust action against employees. Pastors may isolate and hound out innocent members of their congregations. We may be the victims of spouses, in-laws, friends, employers or pastors, but we may also be the unfaithful ones: the spouse with the wandering eye, the resentful son-in-law, the treacherous friend, the lazy and dishonest employee or the obstructive church member.

- *How have you been a victim of unfaithfulness?*

- *How have you been a perpetrator of unfaithfulness?*

How then we must rejoice that God's love is different from the love we receive from other people and that we give to them. He will never be unfaithful, turn against us, act unjustly towards us or hound us out. God is both a lover and a rock. These two biblical images come powerfully together to provide us with a wonderful confidence that God is not and can never be mutable in his love. He will not suddenly cast us off for another.

It is not just that God has decided to be faithful; it is that in his very triune being he is faithful. This is who he is in his own inner relations. He cannot be otherwise. His faithfulness is as certain as his existence. In the covenant of redemption the persons of the Trinity bind themselves to each other to save, so God's covenant faithfulness is as certain as the faithfulness of the Father to his Son, the Son to his Father. God's saving love is as sure as God is God.

The love of God will stand when all else fails, because God always stands. Grasping this is particularly important for us when we face trials in our lives, or when even our lives themselves become a trial to us. These are the times when all other props have been removed and we see clearly what is actually always true: that God is the only rock we have. In a striking letter Robert Murray M'Cheyne wrote to a bereaved friend urging him to find in Christ what cannot be found anywhere else, making this connection between the changelessness of God and our comfort in adversity:

> How sweet, that *Jesus ever liveth*. He is the same yesterday, and to-day, and for ever. You will never find Jesus so precious as when the world is one vast howling wilderness. Then he is like a rose blooming in the midst of the desolation – a rock rising above the storm.[19]

Everything created can be lost. Sometimes other people fail us along the way because they are unfaithful, but even faithful spouses and friends one day die. All our material wealth can be taken from us in an instant. The rich man's investments evaporate overnight as the markets plummet. And even if we hold on to the wealth, it proves ultimately powerless against the bitter realities of human existence. Blessed with a comfortable upbringing, I know the feeling of riding high in a Range Rover or close to the ground in a British sports car, but all the feelings of success, status and security money brings evaporate in the face of illness and death as it proves powerless to help us. All the sparkling baubles are grey beside Jesus. He alone is the bright rose in the midst of a wasteland, because he alone stands through any tempest. God is uniquely faithful in life, in death and beyond the grave.

- *What else do you trust in apart from God?*

- *How will those people or things fail you?*

---

19. Letter of 9 Mar. 1843, in Andrew Bonar, *Memoir and Remains of the Rev. Robert Murray M'Cheyne*, 2nd ed. (Dundee: William Middleton, 1852), p. 291 (italics original).

- *Renouncing your idols, consciously embrace Jesus as the only rose in the wilderness.*

Prayer

'Lord God, you are the creator of space and time, unbounded by place or date. Your triune life is for ever complete. You never gain what you lack or lose what you have. You do not change in who you are or in what you do. Your triune love is for ever perfect. You are faithful to your covenants, always keeping your word. Your purposes are as sure as your existence.

'You are not a man that you should change your mind, yet you stoop to speak to me in the language of a man among men. You invite me to ask you to change your mind, and you do, just as you planned.

'I confess with shame that I am so different from you. I am both the victim and the perpetrator of unfaithfulness, surrounded by it within and without.

'All praise to you, the triune God of faithfulness! In the howling wilderness open my eyes to find in Jesus the rose blooming amid the desolation, the rock rising above the storm. When all else fails, may I find in him my only true circumstance. In his name. Amen.'

9. LOVE WITHOUT PASSION

Passionless psychopaths

In the summer of 1979 the song 'I Don't Like Mondays' by the Boomtown Rats was a UK number one hit single for a month. Bob Geldof wrote the song after he heard the news that 16-year-old Brenda Spencer had killed two adults and wounded eight children and a police officer in a shooting spree at Grover Cleveland Elementary School in San Diego. When police surrounded Spencer's house, from which she had shot at the school across the street, she told a negotiator, 'It was a lot of fun seeing children shot.'[1] When a reporter asked her why she had committed the crime, she replied, 'I don't like Mondays. This livens up the day.'[2]

---

1. 'Parole Denied in School Shooting', *USA Today*, 19 June 2001, http://www.usatoday.com/news/nation/2001-04-18-spencer.htm (accessed 25 July 2012).

2. Robert M. Regoli, John D. Hewitt and Matt DeLisi, *Delinquency in Society*, 8th ed. (Sudbury, Mass.: Jones & Bartlett, 2010), p. 162.

Spencer's answer typifies the detached indifference of a psychopath. One of the leading experts on psychopathy is Robert Hare, who describes a psychopath as 'a self-centred, callous, and remorseless person profoundly lacking in empathy and the ability to form warm emotional relationships with others, a person who functions without the restraints of conscience'.[3] Psychopaths, Hare explains, are not mad: 'Their acts result not from a deranged mind but from a cold, calculating rationality combined with a chilling inability to treat others as thinking, feeling human beings.'[4]

I do not wish to multiply examples of the extraordinary evil of notorious psychopaths, and I hardly need to: most detective novels, television series and films seem at the moment to feature at least one psychopathic serial killer, often too disturbing to watch. The profusion of fictional psychopaths surely risks making all of us a little more like them, casually indifferent to the brutality of their crimes that appear on our screens evening by evening. It will suffice to observe that callous emotional detachment, an inability to feel for others, is a defining characteristic of psychopaths. Hare argues that while it is a small percentage of psychopaths who become criminals, many of us have suffered at the hands of an unfeeling and manipulative psychopath in the normal course of our lives, for example in our families or at work. We do not need to watch programmes depicting the extremes of psychopathic behaviour to know that there is something deeply wrong with someone who cannot feel for others.

Passionless God?

What, then, are we to make of the classical Christian claim that God is 'without body, parts, or passions', that he is 'impassible'?[5] Sensing

---

3. Robert D. Hare, *Without Conscience: The Disturbing World of the Psychopaths Among Us* (New York: Guildford, 1999), p. 2.

4. Ibid., p. 5.

5. The threefold denial is made in the Thirty-Nine Articles (Article 1) and the Westminster Confession of Faith (2.1).

that emotional insensitivity is an aspect of a sinful disorder may be one of the reasons that many Christians are so uneasy about this denial of passions to God. If I may put it so starkly, should God's impassibility be taken to imply that he is like a psychopath? When he sees our suffering, is he coldly indifferent, impassive and uncaring? This is the conclusion of Jürgen Moltmann, who rejects the classical doctrine because 'the one who cannot suffer cannot love either'. Moltmann insists that the impassible God is 'completely insensitive', 'a loveless being', not God but a stone.[6] In the context Moltmann targets specifically the 'unmoved Mover' of Aristotle, but it is clear that he lumps in with it the traditional Christian doctrine of impassibility.

Such a reading of divine impassibility is immediately belied by the Bible, which speaks of how God's heart recoils within him with love for his people (Hos. 11:8) and how his wrath burns against his enemies like a consuming fire (Heb. 12:29). How then did the idea of a passionless God gain a hearing in Christian theology? It seems unlikely that the great theologians of the first 1900 years of the church, the vast majority of whom believed the doctrine, overlooked the plethora of such verses in the Bible. Is there perhaps more to the idea of divine impassibility than meets the eye? Indeed, there is.

The sovereign, eternal, changeless God is passionless

All that we have seen in the previous chapters about God's being sovereign, timeless and changeless implies that the tradition has been right to teach that he is without passions. The early Christian theologians who first described God as impassible did so in large part to maintain his sovereignty over creation. They believed that someone experiencing a passion necessarily loses his sovereignty. Passions are evoked in us by others, which means we are subject to

---

6. Jürgen Moltmann, *The Crucified God: The Cross of Christ as the Foundation and Criticism of Christian Theology*, tr. R. A. Wilson and John Bowden (Minneapolis: Fortress, 1993), p. 222.

them. The ancient writers worked with a definition of passion that fits well with Max Beerbohm's depiction of Oxford under the irresistible influence of Zuleika Dobson: the students were helpless before her.

It helps us see why the church fathers rejected the idea of passions in God if we recall the fickle gods of Greek and Roman mythology, tossed this way and that by their volatile reactions to events. For example, the story of Homer's *Iliad* results from tumultuous events among the gods, though they are mentioned only in passing in the work itself. Eris the god of discord resented not being invited to the wedding of Peleus and Thetis. In her irritation she threw a golden apple among the guests marked 'For the fairest'. None of the gods would decide which of them should have the apple, but they settled on Paris, the son of the Trojan king Priam, to make the decision. Aphrodite bribed Paris by offering him Helen the wife of Menelaos of Sparta, so he decided that Aphrodite was more beautiful than Hera or Athene. The Trojan War then resulted when he took Helen from Sparta and brought her back to Troy.

The *Iliad* tells the story of a short period during that war, and the *Odyssey* concerns the return of Odysseus after it. Thus the two greatest works of classical literature have their roots in stories of the unruly passions of the gods. Confronted by such tales of gods who combined super-human powers with childish truculence, even some of the pagan monotheists themselves had concluded that the one god must be impassible. Christian theologians have rightly taught that the sovereign God is not buffeted by any such passions.

Like God's sovereignty, his eternity and changelessness also imply impassibility. Passions as we know them occur in moments of time as reactions to particular circumstances that come and go. By contrast, the eternal God is not limited to moments of time or to single sets of circumstances. While human passions ebb and flow with the passage of time and the variation of events, God is always the same. He does not have rising and falling passions. In the previous chapter we concluded from the fact that God is tri-une that he is eternal and changeless; now we conclude from the fact that he is eternal and changeless that he does not have passions as we do.

God is divinely passionate

If it is right to deny human passions to God, how do we avoid Moltmann's conclusion that the impassible God is emotionally cauterized, unfeeling, static and dead like a stone? Why does it not follow that there is in God, dare we say it, a divine psychosis, an inability to feel in response to others?

We may begin by noting that this has never been the picture of God that the doctrine of impassibility at its best has painted. For example, while the early church father Lactantius affirms that God is 'incapable of suffering, unchangeable, incorruptible, blessed, and eternal', he does not conclude that God is emotionally dead like a stone.[7] Rather, he distinguishes 'vicious' affections that God does not have from virtuous ones that he does: 'As to those which belong to virtue, – that is, anger towards the wicked, regard towards the good, pity towards the afflicted, – inasmuch as they are worthy of the divine power, He has affections of His own, both just and true.'[8]

John Owen similarly states bluntly that God does not have affections. He goes so far as to state that it would be 'no less than blasphemy' to think of love as an affection in God, because God is never 'subject to passions'.[9] This sounds like a sweeping denial of anything like emotional life to God, but we need to interpret it in the context of other statements Owen makes. In his comments on the word 'loved' in John 3:16 he affirms that God loves the world 'with such an earnest, intense affection, consisting in an eternal, unchangeable act and purpose of his will, for the bestowing of the

7. Lactantius, *The Divine Institutes*, in Alexander Roberts and James Donaldson (eds.), *Ante-Nicene Fathers*, 10 vols. (Buffalo: Christian Literature, 1885–96; repr. Peabody: Hendrickson, 1995), 2.9, 7:55.

8. Lactantius, *A Treatise on the Anger of God*, in Philip Schaff (ed.), *Nicene and Post-Nicene Fathers*, first series, 14 vols. (Buffalo: Christian Literature, 1886–90; repr. Peabody: Hendrickson, 1994), 16, 7:273.

9. John Owen, *The Death of Death in the Death of Christ*, in William H. Goold (ed.), *The Works of John Owen*, 16 vols. (Edinburgh: Banner of Truth Trust, 1965–8; repr. 1993), 3.8, 10:275.

chiefest good (the choicest effectual love)'.[10] According to Owen, God not only has an affection of love for the world; he has an intense affection.

How does Owen square these seemingly contradictory statements, denying and affirming affections in God? The explanation is that he denies specifically human affections in God, but affirms divine affections. When he states that it is a blasphemy to think of God's love as an affection, he has already narrowed the kind of affection he has in view in his denial. He is answering the question 'Is it an affection in his eternal nature, *as love is in ours?*' He rejects the specific idea that God is subjected to an affection as we are. He is denying human affections in God, not all affections. When he affirms that God has the earnest and intense affection of love for the world, he defines carefully what kind of affection he has in mind: 'an eternal, unchangeable act and purpose of his will'. God has affections in a way that are appropriate to him as God.

In this reasoning Owen provides an excellent example of reading the Bible analogically, a concept I explored in chapter 2. Being different from us, God does not have affections as we do, but he does reveal himself to us by using the language of human affections. While affections are to be affirmed in God because Scripture ascribes them to him, it also shows that they must be understood to be different from human affections. Each passage speaks of God analogically, identifying him at certain points with created realities but never identifying him totally with any one reality. One passage interprets another and together they build our picture of God.

In his comments on John 3:16 Owen thus lets other aspects of the doctrine of God inform and control his understanding of divine affections. He finds the affection of love in God, while locating that affirmation in the context of Scripture's teaching that God is sovereign. Setting the affection of love amid the other divine attributes produces a careful description of uniquely divine affections. We are left understanding that God does love intensely, that he does have affections analogous to our own, but that he has them

---

10. Ibid. 4.2, 10:323.

differently, without time or change or loss of sovereignty, in a way that coheres with who he is.

God is maximally alive

In Owen's affirmation of affections in God we can begin to see why the biblical picture of God does not imply that he is emotionally static and dead. Indeed, the way is open for us to grasp why it entails exactly the opposite view of God as maximally alive.

In our experience more lively things, such as plants, animals and people, change a great deal over time, whereas inanimate stones and rocks and mountains remain largely the same. Perhaps we are conditioned by our experience to identify changelessness with a lack of life, and change with life.

In God the identification is reversed: God is changeless because he is most alive. The reason that God does not change is not that he is dead, but that he is maximally alive and, therefore, has no lack that would leave space for him to change. His life is not unchanging because it is inert, but because it is so full. In the love of the Father for the Son and the Son for the Father, God's life is the most vivid, most radiant, most abundant life there is, and his love is, therefore, the fullest love of all.

As long as we are clear that his passions are not human passions, we can rightly say that God is not the least but the most passionate being. The denial of passions in God is not a denial of passions of every kind, but specifically a denial of passions of a limited, human kind. Understood rightly, God has not less but infinitely more affection than any of his creatures. Nothing could be further from the truth than the idea that the emotional life of God is deficient, like that of a psychopath. The classical Christian doctrine of God holds that God is immeasurably more emotionally alive than any other being. God does not have affections like ours not because he has no affections, but because he has the highest degree of affections, maximally realized. It is because God loves so much that his love is not like a human passion.

Imagine a box full of the wooden bricks children love to play with. Our human life is like a box with only a few bricks in it. At any time some bricks have been removed from the box, some are in the box and some have yet to be put into it. Our present experience is only ever an experience of a limited number of bricks. We experience constant change as the bricks rattle around within the box.

By contrast, God's life is like a box full of all its bricks all the time. There are no bricks that have been removed from the box. There are no bricks to be added to the box. God's present experience is an experience of all of the bricks. He has all of his life all 'at once'. He experiences no change as bricks come and go, and the bricks never rattle around because the box is full. The bricks include the divine affections that are analogous to our emotional states. Because God has all his life at once, his affections do not come and go. They are all present in him, always. The affections of God are maximally alive.

In his essay 'The Art of Fiction' the novelist Henry James describes the work of an author. He discusses the claim that authors should write on the basis of their own experience. This, James argues, is not quite right. It is more that authors should be constantly alert as they live their life, and should use their observations in their writing. They should 'try to be one of the people on whom nothing is lost'.[11] James uses an arresting image to describe how authors should seize on the tiny details of their daily experiences:

> Experience is never limited, and it is never complete; it is an immense
> sensibility, a kind of huge spiderweb of the finest silken threads
> suspended in the chamber of consciousness, and catching every airborne
> particle in its tissue. It is the very atmosphere of the mind; and when the
> mind is imaginative – much more when it happens to be that of a man
> of genius – it takes to itself the faintest hints of life, it converts the very
> pulses of the air into revelations.[12]

I find this picture helpful in thinking about the way in which God exists. Obviously God does not create the world as James suggests

---

11. Henry James, *The Art of Criticism: Henry James on the Theory and the Practice of Fiction*, ed. William Veeder and Susan M. Griffin (Chicago: University of Chicago Press, 1986), p. 173.

12. Ibid., p. 172.

an author should write a book, but the picture serves well as an illustration of how God interacts with what he has created. James depicts the author as an 'immense sensibility', whose consciousness is like a giant spider's web that catches every particle on its threads, missing nothing. This is what God is like: he is not emotionally dead, but maximally sensitive to every tremor of his creation. Every halting whispered prayer prayed to him by the smallest child echoes at full volume through the threads in the chamber of his divine consciousness.

Yet God is far greater than James's author: he is not gathering experiences that come to him in inspiring moments of discovery and generate revelations for him. His experiences are all experiences he has himself authored. He is the author of life itself, whose immense sensibility is always sovereign in its ceaseless and exhaustive interaction with his creation. And his divine experience is never limited. It is always complete, every thread of the divine mind humming eternally with the totality of created tremors.

The fact that God possesses all of his life at once like this does not mean that he has all of these created tremors jumbled together in a chaotic and incoherent emotional mess of confused and conflicting passions. To think that would be to suppose that God experiences his life squashed into a single point of time while we experience our life stretched out along a line. But God's life is not like a spy's microdot, a shrunken version of our temporal existence, reduced to a moment. His life is not immeasurably shorter than ours. Such conceptions again mistake our halting attempts to describe eternity in the language of present-tense simultaneity. Time is not brief for God: he is time*less*. We cannot even ask if his life is like a point or a line: it is neither because it cannot be measured on such a scale.

Meditation

We have seen that the triune God does not have passions as we do, but that in his loving he is nonetheless infinitely more passionate than we are. Indeed, his love is more passionate than ours precisely because he does not have passions as we do: the greatness of his

passions arises from their being different from our passions. We lose
and gain our passions, whereas God has all of his in eternity. It will
be profitable for us to reflect on this description of God's life, to
ponder the greatness of it, and to fall silent before it.

- *Imagine just an hour of your life with all of the diverse things in it and
  your emotional responses to them.*

- *Now imagine God's passionate interaction with each of those things:
  his reaction of wrath, jealousy, pity, mercy, love and delight.*

- *Now multiply that set of reactions across a day, a week, a month,
  a year of your life, your three score years and ten.*

- *Then add in the emotional lives of your loved ones, your congregation,
  your colleagues, the inhabitants of your town, your country, the
  world.*

At some point early on in this exercise, you ceased to be able to
imagine the sheer quantity of emotional life involved.

Large quantities are always hard to imagine. We know this when
we try to grasp what certain well-known numbers signify, both good
and ill. It is, for example, very hard to begin to grasp the horrific
magnitude of the Nazis murdering six million people. In Boston
there is a particularly moving Holocaust memorial that helps visualize
the number. It is made of six glass towers standing in a line, representing six concentration camps. Each tower has four sides and is
open up the middle. A public pathway runs through the bottom of
the towers. On each tower glass numbers are etched, one for each
person who died in the camp. It is one thing to hear the number 'six
million'; it is quite another to walk through six tall towers of glass
and to see all the numbers rising high above you representing six of
the camps. The number begins – just begins, no more – to take shape
before your eyes and mind.

But some quantities always remain beyond any imagining. Such
are the quantities of God's life. We could not even depict one second
worth of God's emotional life with a visual aid. In every second of
our time he interacts perfectly with seven billion different people,

each living out a subtle mix of motives and acts that are opaque even to their own enquiry, but transparent to his. The magnitude of God's emotional life can only leave us in awe.

We cannot know what it is like to love as God loves. Even when we have resurrection bodies on the new earth, our life will be everlasting, not eternal, changeless, sovereign or triune. Some of his attributes are incommunicable to us. They cannot be shared with us even in our future sinless state. That is the effect of divine difference, of the transcendence of God above and beyond his creation. We know God is love, and we understand important things about what that means for us. We find that he is kind and merciful, that he does not treat us as we deserve, that he is like a father and a bridegroom to us. We need not, therefore, embrace the theological approach known as the 'negative way' favoured by some mystics, which allows us to talk only about what God is not. Nevertheless, we cannot know what it is like to be God, to love in a way so different from the way we love. The only way we could know that would be by becoming God and living as him, which we cannot.

Our inability to put ourselves in God's shoes should neither surprise nor trouble us. It ought, however, to be humbling for us. God is not only greater than us in what he does; he is greater than us in who he is. We rightly marvel at his works; we should also wonder at his being. The very fabric of his divine life is unimaginable to us. We know truths about it that he has revealed to us, truths we need to know to be reconciled to him and to live for him. Yet all of our halting conceptions are humbled before the superabundance of his triune existence.

- *Meditate on and wonder at the incomprehensibility of God's emotional life.*

Prayer

'Lord God, you are never subject to passions. Your affections do not come and go as time passes. You are not like the shifting shadows that change. You are sovereign, eternal, unchanging, without passions as we know them.

'Father, Son and Holy Spirit, you live in a perfect unity of love from eternity. Your very life is a life of the most intense affection, forever abundant. You are not unfeeling and dead but more passionate and more alive than anything you have made.

'You interact with all space and time at once and yet you know every hair on our heads and respond to every one of your children's prayers individually. I cannot imagine the greatness of your life, the heights of your passions. I bow before you for who you are, the supremely passionate God of love. In the name of Jesus. Amen.'

10. ALL-KNOWING LOVE

The mob wife

One of the recurring themes of gangster stories is the relationship between the mobster and his wife. At the start of the story one of the sons of the Family, rising in social status because of ill-gotten gain, meets a young woman from an entirely different background. He is from downtown New York; she is from rural New Hampshire. He is the son of the Don, a criminal genius; she is the innocent, refined daughter of a Yankee family.

At the start of the story she is wholly ignorant of the Family's activities. But even though the men studiously avoid discussing 'business' with the women, as the tale unfolds she suspects more and more. She cannot help but notice the way people approach the Don for help in a crisis, the respect with which they treat him and the way their intractable problems seem suddenly to be solved. She is intimidated by the powerful aura of the men and their lieutenants. As the conflict of mob families intensifies, the bloodshed comes closer to home and can no longer be hidden or ignored. Gradually she realizes the seriousness of the Family's crimes and the lengths to which the Don will go. Perhaps her husband never hurts her; in his home he is always gentlemanly and gracious, benevolent and warm. But she knows he is a different man outside the home.

Just as the husband is, at least initially, ambiguous to the wife, so she is often ambiguous to the reader or viewer. We are never exactly sure how much she has understood. How far is she guilty by association? In some stories the self-deception is wilful as the wife hides from the facts for as long as she can in order to protect herself, her marriage and her children. Now that she knows what her husband is like, she is afraid to leave him. The more apparent his crimes become, the more strain is placed on the couple. She may stay in the marriage, but it becomes a relationship of necessity in which she is trapped, not one in which she delights. Her knowledge and love are inversely proportional: the more she knows of her husband and his evil, the less she loves him.

God knows everything

God knows everything. He knows the tiny details of creation, even the number of hairs on our heads (Matt. 10:30). He does not know us from afar as a detached observer; he knows us inside out because he created us. He formed our inward parts, knitted us together, intricately wove us in the depths of the earth (Ps. 139:13–16). He does not just know things in the present; he declares 'the end from the beginning' (Isa. 46:10). Nor does he know only what can be deduced from the present state of affairs by a supremely clever being; he knows even the future that depends on myriad human choices. For example, he knows how long we will live, because he has decided it:

> in your book were written, every one of them,
>> the days that were formed for me,
>> when as yet there was none of them.
> (Ps. 139:16)

He knows the times and places of our lives, because he has appointed them: 'he made from one man every nation of mankind to live on

all the face of the earth, having determined allotted periods and the
boundaries of their dwelling place' (Acts 17:26). He knows our
desires and inclinations, because he brings them about:

> The king's heart is a stream of water in the hand of the LORD;
>> he turns it wherever he will.
>
> (Prov. 21:1)

The Bible extends this picture of divine knowledge and control
to include even evil acts, for example the hostility of the pagan
kings to the Hebrews in the exodus, as Moses reports: 'Sihon the king
of Heshbon would not let us pass by him, for the LORD your God
hardened his spirit and made his heart obstinate, that he might give
him into your hand, as he is this day' (Deut. 2:30).

Without becoming responsible for it, God maintains an exhaustive sovereignty over evil. Considering an evil thing in itself, God
does not desire it: he is 'of purer eyes than to see evil' (Hab. 1:13).
Considering the suffering of the lost, he does not want any to perish:
'Have I any pleasure in the death of the wicked, declares the Lord
GOD, and not rather that he should turn from his way and live?'
(Ezek. 18:23). Yet at the same time, God tells us that he makes not
only well-being but also 'calamity' (Isa. 45:7). We even read that he
hardens hearts and does desire death. The same verb used to describe
God's not willing death in Ezekiel 18:23 is used of his willing it for
Hophni and Phinehas, the sons of Eli: 'they would not listen to the
voice of their father, for it was the will of the LORD to put them to
death' (1 Sam. 2:25).[1]

There is mystery here: not the mystery of the compatibility of
libertarian human free will and divine sovereignty (since we have no
such free will as fallen creatures bound in sin and death), but the
mystery of the compatibility of divine sovereignty and human
responsibility. I do not pretend to be able to fathom the mystery,

---

1. As pointed out by John Piper in 'Are There Two Wills in God?',
   in Thomas R. Schreiner and Bruce A. Ware (eds.), *Still Sovereign:
   Contemporary Perspectives on Election, Foreknowledge, and Grace* (Grand
   Rapids: Baker, 2000), p. 117. The verb is *ḥāpēṣ* (to desire).

but the exhaustive extent of God's knowledge and its foundation in his sovereign will are clear: God knows everything, because he wills everything. This is what the proud king Nebuchadnezzar came to see when God humbled him:

> his dominion is an everlasting dominion,
>   and his kingdom endures from generation to generation;
> all the inhabitants of the earth are accounted as nothing,
>   and he does according to his will among the host of heaven
>   and among the inhabitants of the earth;
> and none can stay his hand
>   or say to him: 'What have you done?'
> (Dan. 4:34–35)

In similarly comprehensive tones the apostle Paul speaks of 'the purpose of him who works all things according to the counsel of his will' (Eph. 1:11). God knows all because he wills all.

God knows the extent of our sin

We are sometimes mysterious to one another. Even in close marriages there are still surprises. Sometimes we are even mysterious to ourselves. We awake in a state of mind we cannot explain. We react in a way that frustrates us. And we do not even know ourselves well enough to know what we are doing wrong. In one sense we know our sin all too well, in that it weighs upon us and we cannot evade it; think of David's prayer after his adultery with Bathsheba:

> I know my transgressions,
>   and my sin is ever before me.
> (Ps. 51:3)

His conscience had a painfully clear sense of sin.

But in another sense we do not know our sins, in that we have not grasped the sinfulness of much of what we do. This is not just because we do not know the law of God perfectly; it is also because we do not have a clear sight of our own motives. The same David who saw his sin before him could also confess his ignorance:

> Who can discern his errors?
>   Declare me innocent from hidden faults.
> (Ps. 19:12)

God can declare us innocent of all our sins because they are not hidden to him. He perfectly discerns the extent of our evil, and sees behind our outward words and deeds into the hidden recesses of all our darkened thoughts, our twisted desires and warped loves. It is a frightening thought that God knows us better than we know ourselves.

Only God knows the depth of our sin

God not only knows the numerical quantity of our sins; he also perfectly measures their moral deficiency, the magnitude of their evil. Indeed, only he knows how far short of his glory we have fallen. God's knowledge of the depth of our sin is related to his knowledge of the height of his own glory, since sin's evil consists in being an offence against his divine person. Only God knows himself perfectly, so only he can measure the evil of a sin committed against him.

If we truly knew each other, it would be very hard for us to love each other. If we truly knew ourselves, it would be very hard for us to go on. It would be a constant struggle to endure ourselves, requiring a stronger grasp of God's forgiveness than we already have. We would see the sins we do not see, but more importantly we would see the magnitude and true ugliness of all our sins. We would recognize their full horror against the background of God's goodness. How would we not then be filled with the utmost revulsion? Yet God sees all this, and he sees it with perfect clarity. God thus has a unique knowledge of both the breadth and depth of our sin. With a perfect grasp of who we are, he surely has the greatest reason not to love us.

God's knowledge and his holiness

Our predicament does not just arise from God's knowledge, but also from his holiness. It is the coexistence of God's exhaustive knowledge with his perfect holiness that threatens us. The human relationships in gangster stories illustrate the difficulty when even relative good and evil come together. The starting point for the tension in a mob marriage is the moral difference between the characters. The wife begins the story as an innocent, whereas the husband begins as a man born into crime. Her horror at his crimes arises from the contrast between them. The reason that she loves less the more she knows is that she is so different from him. In some versions the final tragedy comes when the marked difference is eroded and finally erased. The wife becomes like her husband, driven to crime to protect her family, ending with blood on her own hands. Now she cannot condemn because she herself is compromised.

God is never compromised. He has none of his own sin to reduce him to our level. When he knows our sin, there is nothing about his own life that would leave him humbled alongside us. In his holy being he is most highly sensitized to sin. He 'cannot look at wrong' (Hab. 1:13). God zealously maintains his holy difference from us. Moses likens him to a consuming fire (Deut. 4:24; cited in Heb. 12:29), burning up wickedness like a blaze through dry brush. As John Owen comments, his zeal is controlled – God is 'rational and intelligent fire' – but it is nonetheless implacable by any creature.[2] God has no sin of his own to compromise or temper his reaction to ours. Given his holiness, we might rightly expect him to cast the entire human race into hell.

God's surprising compassion

God sees us with perfect clarity. Revulsion arises in his holy nature

---

2. John Owen, *A Dissertation on Divine Justice*, in William H. Goold (ed.), *The Works of John Owen*, 16 vols. (Edinburgh: Banner of Truth Trust, 1965–8; repr. 1993), 10.603.

as he regards us in our sin. But still, even as God knows all our evil deeds and hates them, he loves us. The more we know of evil, the less we are inclined to love. The more God knows of our evil, as much as he hates it, the more he seeks us out. His mercy on his people rises above his wrath. Even as the consuming fire of his holy being burns against us, he loves us. Here are the breathtaking words of Psalm 78 about God's mercy on a persistently rebellious Israel:

> They remembered that God was their rock,
> the Most High God their redeemer.
> But they flattered him with their mouths;
> they lied to him with their tongues.
> Their heart was not steadfast towards him;
> they were not faithful to his covenant.
> Yet he, being compassionate,
> atoned for their iniquity
> and did not destroy them;
> he restrained his anger often
> and did not stir up all his wrath.
> He remembered that they were but flesh,
> a wind that passes and comes not again.
> (vv. 35–39)

Psalm 103 expresses the same idea:

> As a father shows compassion to his children,
> so the LORD shows compassion to those who fear him.
> For he knows our frame;
> he remembers that we are dust.
> (vv. 13–14)

We might expect exactly the opposite of what these psalms say: that seeing how weak we are and what a mess we have made of our lives, God would simply cast us off. But instead we read that his knowledge of who we are stirs his compassion. God remembers our weak constitution, that we are but flesh, a momentary wind, dust. He understands our vulnerability as frail creatures and responds with love. Gregory the Great reflects that this awareness of human frailty may be part of the reason why God has mercy on fallen human beings but not fallen angels:

> When the Creator took compassion to work redemption, it was meet that He should bring back to Himself that creature, which, in the commission of sin, plainly had something of infirmity; and it was also meet that the apostate Angel should be driven down to a farther depth, in proportion as he, when he fell from resoluteness in standing fast, carried about him no infirmity of the flesh.[3]

God's universal compassion

How extensive is God's compassion? My attention in this book is focused on God's effective, saving love for his bride the church. Nonetheless, it is important to note that God's general compassion extends beyond his chosen people to every human being, all of whose sin he knows. When God speaks through Ezekiel to call Israel to repentance, he states clearly, 'I have no pleasure in the death of anyone' (18:32). He shows his universal love by providing for the needs of all his creatures:

> The LORD is good to all,
>   and his mercy is over all that he has made.
> (Ps. 145:9)

God does not restrict his providential blessings to his chosen people: 'he makes his sun rise on the evil and on the good, and sends rain on the just and on the unjust' (Matt. 5:45). Jesus made this point to teach his disciples that they should love their enemies, so he evidently thought that God's providential care for all was identifiable as an instance of his love. And Jesus himself showed compassion on the perishing as well as the saved. He looked at the rich young man, who

---

3. Gregory the Great, *Morals on the Book of Job*, ed. Paul A. Böer, 3 vols. (n.p.: Veritatis Splendor, 2012), 1:160.

as far as we know never surrendered his riches, and 'loved him' (Mark 10:21). He wept over Jerusalem as he warned of its destruction (Luke 19:41). And he himself kept the moral law perfectly, which must mean that he loved all his neighbours, not just his disciples (Matt. 22:39). God's compassion extends to all his creatures.

Pity for the victim

The common grace God shows to all people is not what any deserve. Still less do any merit the saving grace by which he effectually redeems his chosen people. Part of the reason for God's effective, saving pity is that while he knows our sin he also knows that we have not ended up in this situation solely by our own wrongdoing. We need to be careful here because contemporary Western culture loves to magnify the victim. Let me be clear: Adam was responsible for his sin, and we are responsible for our sin in him (Rom. 5:12–21), and for the sin in our own lives. But there is also a sense in which we are indeed the vulnerable victims of the devil's attack. Eve was deceived by him (1 Tim. 2:14), and in our fallen state we are all alike trapped by him, unable to break free. We are guilty perpetrators, but also tragic victims.

God pities us in our powerlessness. Imagine a small girl, failing to master her temper, overreacting when a drawing she is doing goes wrong. Her father is cross with her, but he also feels for her childish weakness. This is how God sees us. He sees both our culpable lack of self-control and our pitiable weakness before the onslaught of Satan. A mighty fallen angel has taken us captive. We have been overcome by a terrible enemy whose natural powers far exceed those of any mere man.

Gregory again finds a reason here for the different ways God reacts to the fall of Satan and the fall of man: we fell by the wickedness of another, whereas Satan fell solely by his own wickedness.[4] God sees the devil enslaving us and hates the evil done against us. He sends one to fight for us who is fully man but more than a man, the Lord Jesus Christ. It is he who comes to do what we could never

---

4. Ibid.

do, to bind the strong man Satan and to plunder his house (Mark 3:27). We are the treasure he takes. God alone measures our sin; he alone hates it as it should be hated, and yet he alone comes in Christ to set us free from Satan.

Longsuffering love

God's love is also remarkable because it is longsuffering in the face of human sin. We live in an age of rapidly dissolved relationships. Celebrity divorces can be notoriously rapid, with some marriages lasting just days or hours. By contrast, God endures centuries of disobedience from his people and yet perseveres in love for them. He is patient with his enemies, waiting while Noah built the ark before sending the flood (1 Peter 3:20), and for hundreds of years while the sin of the Amorites built up before sending his people against them (Gen. 15:16). He gave the pharaoh repeated opportunities to release the Hebrews before sending more plagues and finally taking the firstborn of Egypt (Exod. 5 – 12). Until the coming of Christ and the publishing of the gospel, God overlooked the 'times of ignorance' among the nations (Acts 17:30), and 'passed over former sins' (Rom. 3:25).

God is patient not only with his enemies but especially with his own people. When Yahweh reveals his name to Moses in the wilderness, he tells him he is 'slow to anger' (Exod. 34:6), a Hebrew expression literally denoting being 'long nosed', most likely a metaphor for being slow to flare his nostrils in anger. In the wilderness he 'put up with them' for forty years (Acts 13:18). Peter writes that God now waits patiently for his people to come to repentance: 'The Lord is not slow to fulfil his promise as some count slowness, but is patient towards you, not wishing that any should perish, but that all should reach repentance' (2 Peter 3:9). The Greek word for 'patient' here is a compound of words for 'long' and 'anger', like the word for being long-nosed in the Old Testament it was used to translate. God is long in restraining his anger. Even as we stagger on in sin and God knows it inside out, he is patient. His patience does not, however, last for ever. Peter continues, 'But the day of the Lord will come like a thief' (2 Peter 3:10).

Known by God and still known by God

We have been considering God's knowledge of us in the sense of his complete awareness of the facts about who we are and what we are like. But when the Bible speaks of God's knowledge, it often means more than that he knows everything *about* us. The deeper sense of knowledge in Scripture refers to God's knowing us not only factually, but also relationally. His relational knowledge obviously presumes his factual knowledge, but it goes beyond it. When Jesus prays to his Father saying, 'this is eternal life, that they know you the only true God, and Jesus Christ whom you have sent' (John 17:3), he is obviously not describing a merely factual knowledge; he is referring to a living relationship with God.

The wonder of God's love for us is revealed clearly when we juxtapose these two ways in which the Bible speaks about the knowledge of God. God has an exhaustive factual knowledge of us, including the depth and breadth of our sin. And yet, with that in full view, he also has an intimate relational knowledge of his reconciled people. The two kinds of divine knowledge in Scripture – factual and relational – thus provide a way of expressing the wonder of God's knowing love: God knows us, and yet he still wills to know us.

Nor is God a reluctant partner in this relationship. In his compassion he always takes the first step, drawing close to know us relationally before he draws us close to know him. Like his grace, his knowledge prevenes ours. Not only does he take the initiative; he also enters more deeply into the relationship than we do, knowing us with a depth our own knowledge of him cannot yet possess.

The Bible generally speaks more about our knowing God than it does about his knowing us, but it does speak about people being known by him at some key moments.[5] For example, before the destruction of Sodom and Gomorrah we are given this remarkable window into God's mind:

---

5. I have been helped on this neglected theme by Brian S. Rosner, '"Known by God": The Meaning and Value of a Neglected Biblical Concept', *Tyndale Bulletin* 59.2 (2008), pp. 207–230.

> Shall I hide from Abraham what I am about to do, seeing that
> Abraham shall surely become a great and mighty nation, and all the
> nations of the earth shall be blessed in him? For I have known him,
> that he may command his children and his household after him to
> keep the way of the LORD by doing righteousness and justice, so
> that the LORD may bring to Abraham what he has promised him.
> (Gen. 18:17–19)[6]

God's knowledge of Abraham stood as the foundation of his purpose to bless him, and through him all the nations of the earth. When Moses intercedes with God, he pleads the fact that God said to him, 'I know you by name' (Exod. 33:12). When the Lord calls Jeremiah to his ministry, he tells him, 'Before I formed you in the womb I knew you' (Jer. 1:5). According to Amos, it is the Lord's knowledge of Israel that increases her responsibility for her sin and brings on her his judgment:

> You only have I known
>   of all the families of the earth;
> therefore I will punish you
>   for all your iniquities.
> (Amos 3:2)

These examples all show the importance of God's knowledge of his people; it is the basis of his redemptive plan, of his people's hope and assurance, and of his judgment.

In the New Testament Jesus warns that on the day of judgment he will send away with the words 'I never knew you' even some who have done great miracles (Matt. 7:23). He describes his sheep in terms of what they do – they 'hear my voice' and 'follow me' – but punctuates this with a statement about his knowledge of them: 'and I know them' (John 10:27). The apostle Paul indicates that being known by God is more fundamental than knowing him. He writes to the Galatians:

---

6. I have used the translation of *yd'* given in the footnotes of the English Standard Version rather than the main text's 'I have chosen'.

> Formerly, when you did not know God, you were enslaved to those that
> by nature are not gods. But now that you have come to know God, or
> rather to be known by God, how can you turn back again to the weak
> and worthless elementary principles of the world, whose slaves you
> want to be once more? (Gal. 4:8–9)

Why does Paul think that it is more accurate to describe the transition
from slaves to sons as coming to be known by God than coming to
know him? The answer may be found in his vision of glory in 1 Corinthians: 'Now I know in part; then I shall know fully, even as I have
been fully known' (13:12). Paul implies that we do not yet know God
fully. Whenever we speak of our knowledge of God, we are speaking
of something partial. Later, in glory, we will attain to a full knowledge of God, but we do not have it yet. By contrast, God already
knows us fully. God's knowledge of us is complete; our knowledge
of him is incomplete. Our conversion, therefore, may more properly
be described as God's coming to know us than as our coming to
know him, since his knowledge is more complete than ours.

There is an asymmetry of knowledge in the divine–human relationship during this life. The knowledge is mutual – God knows us
and we know him – but it is not equal. The inequality arises because
God's knowledge of us is the basis for our knowledge of him. Before
Jeremiah knew God, God knew Jeremiah. We cannot come to know
God unless he first wills to draw near to us and to draw us near to him.
Even then, our knowledge of God will not be complete until we are
entirely renewed in the final resurrection and dwell with him on the
new earth. Then, with sight clear of sin, we will know as we are known.

We have seen that God knows us inside out, and yet has compassion
on us. He knows all about us, and yet he wills to know us as our covenant God. More than that, he takes the initiative in knowing us. His
knowledge is always first. And it is his knowledge of us that provides
the basis of our imperfect, yet-to-be-fulfilled knowledge of him.

Meditation

How remarkable to add to the picture of God as a consuming fire
the image of a compassionate father stooping tenderly to his frail

children! Consider how wonderful it is that even as God's holiness burns against sinners, he also looks upon us with the deepest pity and patience. Isaiah saw the blazing glory of Jesus in the temple (John 12:41), but it is this same Jesus who provided the burning coal that cleansed his lips (Isa. 6:6–7), and of whom Isaiah prophesied:

> a bruised reed he will not break,
>   and a faintly burning wick he will not quench.
> (42:3)

What a beautiful thing it is to see alongside each other God's holiness and his compassion, his zeal against sin and the vast pity in his heart.

- *Given that God knows you inside out, what does he know about you?*

- *Standing on your own two feet, what would you deserve from God's hand?*

- *Now spend time wondering at how God actually treats you on the basis of his compassion.*

We can reflect further on the wonder of God's knowing love by meditating on the two ways in which he knows us: factually and relationally. There is an extraordinary liberty and joy in realizing that we are known exactly as we are and yet are still drawn into and held in relationship with God. The thought of being fully known with no secrets is initially very alarming and shames us, but it comes to be delightful. Like a man standing on the brink of a chilly freshwater pond, we hesitate to think of being fully known, but when once we are in the water the experience is bracing. The delight is the delight of being accepted just as we are by one who cannot be surprised by the extent of our sin. Some people may love us because they do not know what we are really like. Some may know more of what we are like and labour still to love us. Others who know may reject us. God is like none of these.

Before the eyes of God there is no need for us to make out that we are what we are not. He does not need to work hard to love us. There is no need to fear that God will discover how bad we really are and change his mind about loving us. God can never discover anything about us that will turn him against us, because he can never discover anything about us at all. All that we have been, all that we are, all that we will be is naked before his eye from eternity. Nothing about us, no matter how bad, ever surprises God. He sees straight through our cultivated veneer of righteousness. We are utterly transparent to him. He sees both the number and the depth of all of our sins. And still he loves us, still he graciously draws close to us and draws us close to him.

- *What would you most fear someone finding out about you? What would they think of you if they discovered it?*

- *Have you experienced someone finding something out about you and choosing not to love or like you?*

- *Reflect on the wonderful coexistence of God's complete factual knowledge of your sin and his abiding love for you.*

Having been treated like this, we must surely be provoked to treat others likewise. There are few things uglier than the servant in the parable who, having been forgiven a debt of ten thousand talents by the king, demands full payment of just a hundred denarii from his fellow servant (Matt. 18:21–35). This is a man who has forgotten that he himself is a forgiven sinner. I can always find someone whose sins are more serious than mine, someone whose example provides me with the secret comfort that I am not *that* bad. When a friend confesses to me about some sin that burdens him, what is my reaction? Is it to think that I am in a different category from him because he is the one confessing, while I am the one being confessed to? God alone is in a different category. We always stand beside other sinners as ones who are alike guilty before a holy God. We are always to measure ourselves not against someone else's sins on a scale of relative guilt, but against the absolute scale of God's holiness. If there is a moment of pride in being different, then we are like the Pharisee looking down on the tax collector (Luke 18:9–14). If the holy God who has no sin reacts with pity to us, then how much more should we react with pity to others.

- *In which relationships are you most tempted to locate yourself above others in a pecking order of holiness?*

- *With those relationships in mind reflect on your own need for forgiveness and the depths from which you have been saved.*

Prayer

'Heavenly Father, I praise you for your perfect knowledge of all things. You know them because you planned and created them. You know me inside out: every hair on my head, every one of my days. You know me better than I know myself.

'I tremble to think that you know my sins. When I think of the ways in which I have sinned I am horrified, but I know that I am not as horrified as I should be because I do not see the extent of my guilt clearly. You see my sins for what they are, measured against your holiness that you alone know perfectly. You burn against my sins with holy zeal. Seeing me as an evildoer, you rightly hate me.

'Yet in your grace you look on me with pity and patience. You know that I am flesh, wind and dust. You know my frame and are kind to me. You know me for what I am, and yet you still will to know me intimately as your child.

'Lord Jesus, you are thrice holy. You are the ruin of sinners who come into your presence unforgiven, and yet you do not break a bruised reed or quench a smouldering wick. You hate sin and sinners, yet you laid down your life to forgive me. You saw me bound by Satan, and you set me free by binding him.

'Holy Spirit, you are the Lord and search the depths of God. You are symbolized by purifying fire and an innocent dove. You are grieved by all evil. And yet you have come to live in me, making my body a temple in which you dwell.

'Lord God, make me more like you. Forgive me when I treat others with a harshness that you have spared me. Help me to show mercy to others as you have shown mercy to me. In your name. Amen.'

Indulgent love

Having considered the pity of God for sinners, we may be left troubled by questions about his justice. If he knows the facts of who we are, how can he know us relationally without compromising his holiness? How can God have pity on us if he is a consuming fire? If his eyes are too pure even to behold evil, how can he have anything to do with people like us? Does he just indulge us, like a parent spoiling a naughty child? Does he wink at evil?

Human love is often indulgent. Recently there was a remarkable programme on British television called *The World's Strictest Parents*. Each episode featured two British families with an out-of-control teenage child. Typically the child was seen swilling vodka, smoking marijuana, swearing at his parents and expressing his determination not to change. The parents were seen despairing of him, or at least the mother was, since she was often on her own. They feared for his future, and wished he would change. At the same time, they took no effective steps towards disciplining him. They moaned, but drew no fixed lines. They shouted, but no calm, measured punishment was imposed. Invariably it was the parents' own money that funded the teen's drinking and drug-taking, and we saw them dishing out £10 notes as he headed out for a long evening's partying.

Do these parents love their children? I have no doubt they do. Their choked voices and tears said as much. Despite any momentary bravado for the cameras, they took no pleasure in the mess in which their family found itself. But the indulgence of the parents was ruining the child. In the rest of the programme the two teens flew to another country to live with a stricter family (which often turned out to be a Christian one). Usually just a few days of clear boundaries and punishments calmly imposed had a transformative effect on them. They returned home to apologize to their parents and to seek a fresh start, which, from the follow-up programme, appeared often to last.

Is God a hypocrite?

The families seen in each episode of this programme show the difference between a love that is indulgent and one that insists on maintaining the distinction between right and wrong. The parents ought to have maintained the boundaries they set, and to have imposed the punishments they threatened, but they failed to do so. Clearly they had gone too far in their laissez-faire parenting. The families that the children stayed with overseas ran their homes with much more consistent discipline.

While parents should discipline their children, even a perfect parent would not punish every wrongdoing. Parents should discipline their children, but they do not do so because they are the arbiters of justice. They discipline to correct, not to satisfy justice. Christian individuals have even more cause to overlook sins committed against them by their neighbours, since it is not their job to correct them. In the Sermon on the Mount Jesus teaches, 'I say to you, Do not resist the one who is evil. But if anyone slaps you on the right cheek, turn to him the other also' (Matt. 5:39). From such verses we conclude that love requires of us accepting injury and not seeking retribution or payback for offences committed against us. While there is certainly such a thing as being overindulgent in parenting, no human relationship should proceed on the basis of punishing every sin.

What about God? Some preachers and theologians wrongly conclude from the teaching of the Sermon on the Mount that God himself must not punish sins committed against him, because he tells us not to punish sins committed against us. Just like us, he must not seek payment for sin; just like us, he must forego punishing. This claim has dramatic consequences when it works its way through a theology. It leads, for example, to the conclusion that when Jesus died on the cross, he could not have been bearing the punishment for our sins. If Jesus did bear punishment from God, then God would be a hypocrite because while telling us not to seek retribution he sought it himself.

Steve Chalke expresses this objection to penal substitutionary atonement: 'If the cross has anything to do with penal substitution then Jesus' teaching becomes a divine case of "do as I say, not as I do." I, for one, believe that God practices what he preaches!'[1] This position presumes that love must mean for God what it means for us. God himself tells us that love for us means not seeking retribution; therefore love must mean that for him too. If he does not conform to what he requires of us, he is the divine hypocrite.

The apostle Paul on the divine difference

Such an argument presumes that divine and human love can be identified in their relationship to retribution. It fails to grasp that they are compared analogically in Scripture. The Bible does not identify divine and human love in how they relate to retribution; it distinguishes them. Nowhere does Scripture suggest that God is like us in that he refuses to permit himself retribution against sin. Certainly there are texts, a glorious number of them, that tell us he

---

1. Steve Chalke, 'Cross Purposes', *Christianity*, Sept. 2004, p. 47. Whatever ambiguity there may have been in his original statements in *The Lost Message of Jesus* (co-authored with Alan Mann), Chalke's position on penal substitutionary atonement was made crystal clear in this article.

forgives sin. But no text claims he forgives without also seeking satisfaction for sin.

In fact, the apostle Paul himself argues the exact opposite from Chalke, underlining how different God and man are in just this respect. In a passage where he tellingly echoes the teaching of Jesus in the Sermon on the Mount, he draws a marked and unmistakable distinction between God and the Christian. What is more, he explains that we are to behave one way precisely because God behaves differently:

> If possible, so far as it depends on you, live peaceably with all. Beloved, never avenge yourselves, but leave it to the wrath of God, for it is written, 'Vengeance is mine, I will repay, says the Lord.' (Rom. 12:18–19, quoting Deut. 32:35)

See Paul's logic here: you must not take revenge, because God will. God is different from us.

We may still wonder why this does not make God a hypocrite. How can it be right for God to command us to do one thing and yet do the opposite himself? It is not hard to find the explanation in the text. Paul quotes words spoken in Deuteronomy by the Lord, Yahweh, the covenant God of Israel. In the passage from which he cites, Yahweh identifies himself as the only God:

> See now that I, even I, am he,
>   and there is no god beside me;
> I kill and I make alive;
>   I wound and I heal;
>   and there is none that can deliver out of my hand.
> (32:39)

The point is clear: God alone can take vengeance, because he alone is God. He is not bound by what he requires of us because he is not one of us. Given that God alone is God, so infinitely greater than we are and standing in a different place with regard to the rest of creation, it is obvious that he should behave differently from us.

Asking why God does not have to do what we have to do is like asking why the owner of a restaurant chain wears a suit but the chef wears an apron, or why a father can tend the fire in the hearth but his young child cannot. Perhaps more relevant to Paul's argument is the example of a victim and a judge. If the victim of a crime were to abduct the criminal and imprison him in his basement, he would be guilty of kidnapping. But if a judge sentences a thief to prison, he acts justly. The definition of what is right and wrong for us varies depending on who we are, on the office we hold. It is not difficult to see why the creator God of the universe, its moral governor and judge, should act differently from an individual Christian person. He stands in a different relation both to every creature and to the law from anyone else.

Does Paul's argument mean that no human should exact any kind of vengeance? Paul is unequivocal: the ordinary Christians to whom he writes are not to take vengeance. But he does then give a limited remit for vengeance to the state:

> Let every person be subject to the governing authorities. For there is no authority except from God, and those that exist have been instituted by God. Therefore whoever resists the authorities resists what God has appointed, and those who resist will incur judgment. For rulers are not a terror to good conduct, but to bad. Would you have no fear of the one who is in authority? Then do what is good, and you will receive his approval, for he is God's servant for your good. But if you do wrong, be afraid, for he does not bear the sword in vain. For he is the servant of God, an avenger who carries out God's wrath on the wrongdoer. (Rom. 13:1–4)

Paul here explains that God has established the governing authorities as his servants to restrain evil and to reward good. It is their role to enact, in the present time and in part, God's wrath against evildoers. Their judgments will always be provisional and limited, but they are allowed, indeed required, to do what an individual Christian is not permitted to do. In Romans 12 – 13 Paul thus mentions three parties: the individual Christian believer who is never to take vengeance, the governing authority who has a limited remit to do so and God himself who will do so perfectly.

What about parents? I began this chapter by describing parents who fail to maintain the difference between right and wrong for their children. Is parental discipline prohibited because God alone exacts retribution? The answer must be that parental discipline is not prohibited, because it is not intended as a means of retribution. No matter how great an offence a child has committed, the punishment inflicted by a parent is not inflicted as a payment for the sin. Parental discipline has in common with retribution that it must be deserved; in that sense it is restrained by the retributive principle. But it is never a means of retribution. It is a dangerous thing indeed when a parent thinks he or she is ministering cosmic justice towards a child. Parental discipline is tightly limited by its aim, which is only and always to correct children, to 'bring them up in the discipline and instruction of the Lord' (Eph. 6:4). It is remedial and reformatory, not retributive.

Justice by substitutionary punishment

Christians should not insist on the demands of justice in their relationships, but God properly does because he is God. The holiness of his being requires him to act justly in bringing his wrath against sin. The question returns: How does he do so? How can he know us relationally without compromising his inherent holiness and the exercise of his justice against sin? How can he act in a way that is consistently both loving and just?

We need to be careful at this juncture not to depict God as conflicted within himself. It is not as if he faces a dilemma he struggles to solve. He does not sit around puzzling over what to do next: 'Oh no! I want to forgive, but – oh dear, how? I want to take sin seriously and to punish it but – um, er, ah, I can't see a way . . . Got it! I know! I'll do it this way . . .'. There has never been such a dilemma for God. The reconciliation of divine love and the demands of divine justice may appear as a dilemma to us, but God has no dilemmas. He does not face problems for which he struggles to find solutions.

I recall from my student days a mathematician friend sitting at his desk staring at a blank piece of paper trying to fathom some deep problem of viscous flows. He would sit for hours on end, sometimes reduced to tears, but occasionally exclaiming for joy as the pieces of the puzzle fell into place all of a sudden. God is not like that. He is never stumped by particularly taxing problems regarding his purposes. He has always, from eternity, existed in the perfect harmony of his love and justice and purposed their integrated outworking in history.

How are they worked out in harmony? At the cross. In its teaching on sacrifice the Bible makes clear that God could either punish us for our sins, or a substitute in our place. The Lord Jesus came as our substitute to die in our place, to bear our sins on the cross, so that God's justice is maintained because our sins are truly punished: 'By sending his own Son in the likeness of sinful flesh and for sin, he condemned sin in the flesh' (Rom. 8:3). This is how love and justice are worked out harmoniously: in the one cross God acts in love to save and in justice to punish.

The cross, the supreme revelation of God's love, shows love working in perfect harmony with his justice. When John explains how we know that 'God is love' (1 John 4:8), he does not speak of God's setting aside the requirements of justice but of his fulfilling them through the offering of the Son: 'In this is love, not that we have loved God but that he loved us and sent his Son to be the propitiation for our sins' (1 John 4:10). As David Wells comments, the love of God 'is not love in general, not just good will, not simply a general benevolence, not an undiscriminating affection, not romantic love, but love whose heart is sacrificial, self-emptying, and whose connections are with what is moral'.[2] According to John, God's love *is* the love that deals with sin.

Punished in Christ

There is forgiveness for us because the just price of our sin is paid by Christ. This is possible because Christ and his people are united. In the covenant of redemption that the Father makes with the Son, the Son is appointed as the head of the church, his body. The union between Christ and his people is thus planned in eternity, so that we

---

2. David F. Wells, *God in the Whirlwind: How the Holy-Love of God Reorients Our World* (Nottingham: Inter-Varsity Press, 2014), p. 86.

are chosen in him before the creation of the world (Eph. 1:3). When the Son of God came in the flesh, therefore, he came already identified as the head of that people. Then in history, as the church grows and people are drawn to Christ, that union becomes an existential reality as the Holy Spirit joins us one by one to the head of the body. The apostles John and Paul especially stress that we are now *in* and *with* Christ. He is the vine and we are the branches; we abide in him and he in us (John 15:5). We died and were buried with him by baptism, being united with him in his death (Rom. 6:3–5).

It is because this union is so close that we can and must say that we died with Christ, as Paul does in 2 Corinthians 5:14: 'one has died for all, therefore all have died'. The union is so close that we can even speak of being punished in him. Here is how John Owen describes it:

> [God] might punish the elect either in their own persons, or in their surety [legal substitute] standing in their room and stead; and when he is punished, they also are punished: for in this point of view the federal head and those represented by him are not considered as distinct, but as one; for although they are not one in respect of personal unity, they are, however, one, – that is, one body in mystical union, yea, *one mystical Christ;* – namely, the surety is the head, those represented by him the members; and when the head is punished, the members also are punished.[3]

Owen explains here how God maintains his love and justice in perfect harmony. The sins of God's people are not left unpunished. They are punished in Christ, to whom Christians are so united as their head that they may be said to be punished for their sins.

This is why Christ's sin-bearing death in our place was possible, because we are so closely united to him, first in the decree, then in his work as our head, and finally in our own lives. Were that union not to exist we might well think that substitution is an injustice since someone unrelated to us would then be punished, but, given our

---

3. John Owen, *A Dissertation on Divine Justice*, in William H. Goold (ed.), *The Works of John Owen*, 16 vols. (Edinburgh: Banner of Truth Trust, 1965–8; repr. 1993), 2.15, 10:598 (italics original).

union, Christ can justly bear our sins. When he does that, God acts in love to save us, and in perfect justice to condemn our sin.

Meditation

The maintenance of the demands of God's justice in his works of love is a vital difference between his love and ours. Unlike other differences that arise from our sinful falling short of his glory, this is a morally vital difference that must be maintained. If we fail to differ from God at this point, we will probably fall into one of two errors.

On the one hand, we might think that because God is like us, he himself must do what he tells us to do. For him to love he must wink at the entire hideous mass of human sin, leaving it unpunished. In this view God will fail to pronounce the 'No' of judgment over sin and sinners. Were God like us in this way his justice would be fatally compromised. Such would be the abandonment of God's justice in this view that it is hard to see how it would not in the end resolve into the idea that all people are saved regardless of their response to Christ.

There is also a more subtle problem with making God like us in this fashion. Those who deny that God will punish think that their teaching will prevent our seeking retribution. They believe that a God who does not punish provides a powerful motive for us not to punish. In fact, their position makes it more likely that you and I will seek our own retribution, because we will in the end seek to provide for ourselves the justice that God himself fails to supply for us. When Paul urges the Roman Christians not to seek vengeance, the basis for his exhortation is that they do not need to because God will do it. They can safely leave it to him. If we teach that God will not exact retribution, then the reason for us not to seek it ourselves evaporates. Paul's logic suggests that the denial of retribution to God will in the end encourage Christians to seek it for themselves.

On the other hand, if we forget this difference between divine and human love, then we may think that we are to be like God by always insisting on retribution. This is a dangerous conceit, since we will find ourselves having to demand punishment for anyone who offends against us. Unlike the Lord, we cannot constitute a mystical head as their substitute, so we will have to pursue every last farthing from any individual who sins against us. See how evil this is: it means making ourselves God, appointing ourselves to be the cosmic ministers of justice. Like Satan, we would put ourselves in the place of God.

We will avoid both noxious alternatives only if we firmly grasp and maintain the difference between God's love and our love in their relations to justice. Then we will honour the justice of God by teaching that he deals with sin and never winks at sinners. Then we will realize that because God always acts in agreement with the demands of his justice we do not have to do so. We will understand that we do not have to seek retribution, to pursue every claim, to fight back against every injustice, to exact every last farthing. We will see, in short, why we can let things go. We will be content with our station and will flee the temptation to take the place of God.

Perhaps you know people who have sought God's place, who have not let go of their demand for justice? They have held on to their claim month after month, year after year, lawyer after lawyer. Perhaps they could have no resort to law, but they have nursed their resentment privately. It is like a treasured pet, cared for, kept warm, fed, watered, nestled in the hay, growing and growing, until it turns around and devours them. What started as a seemingly harmless pet becomes a monster that consumes them, eroding their identity in their maniacal obsession with the one goal of vindication here and now by their own hand. Perhaps you know such a person. Perhaps you are that person.

- *Are you such a person? Do you nurse a desire for revenge? Is it young? Have you harboured it for years?*

It might be a demand for justice from a non-Christian enemy, a persecutor, an employer who objected to your witness for Christ and engineered your removal on some pretext, leaving you without job and home. It might be a demand for justice from a family member, from someone who abused you in some way, perhaps emotional, perhaps physical. Sadly for many Christians it is a demand for justice from a pastor or Christian leader, someone who professed to care but turned out to be a butcher rather than a protector of the sheep, someone who wrongly marked you as an enemy, who isolated you and hounded you out of a church. Part of you longs to expose your enemies, to placard their behaviour on a website for the world to see. Then people will know them for what they are! Some people have never met this temptation. Others live with it day by day. For some it is almost too late. There is little of their former life left apart from the searing desire for revenge.

- *Have you come to that point?*

If that is you, I urge you, in the name of Jesus Christ, to stop. Turn your back on it. Walk away. Let it go. Leave room for the wrath of God. It is, quite simply, none of your business. Retribution is the Lord's work; leave it to him. He is the just ruler of the universe. He is the custodian of rights and wrongs. He will deal with it. Do you trust him to deal with it? Do you think he does not see it, the sin done against you in darkness? Do you think he does not care? That good and evil do not matter to him? Then behold the cross! See there his perfect justice. Know that every sin has either been dealt with on the cross or will be dealt with in hell. Trust him to do it. As you do that, you will find that day by day, with prayers of explicit renunciation, the monster shrinks and finally lies impotent before the transforming power of Christ at work in you. If it lingers, it lingers only as an occasional temptation that has lost its enslaving power. And you will even find that you can follow the example of the Lord Jesus in asking God not to curse your enemies, but to bless them.

- *Consciously let God be God with your grievance in mind.*

- *Bless your enemies.*

Prayer

'Lord God, I bow before you and acknowledge that you are at once merciful and gracious, and the judge of all the earth who will do what is just. You sent your Son the Lord Jesus to lift my sin from me and to bear its punishment in my place. In him you have shown your love and justice in perfect harmony, taking my sin from me, yet not leaving it unpunished.

'Even as I acknowledge you as judge, I confess that I have from time to time sought to take that role upon myself. I have dared to cast myself as the cosmic arbiter, weighing and condemning others as if I were you.

'Forgive me for my presumption in trying to take your place. Forgive my hypocrisy in judging others when I myself deserve judgment.

'Help me to remember that vengeance is yours and not mine. Set me free from the desire for vindication that grips me. Help me to love my enemies. Bless them and do them good. For the sake of Jesus. Amen.'

12. LOVE THAT MAKES THE BELOVED BEAUTIFUL

Loving the lovely

God's love is different from human love because it is a beautifying love. God does not find people who are beautiful and then decide to love them. Rather, he makes the objects of his love beautiful. They owe their beauty to him. Human love can have a beautifying aspect too, for example when a husband desires to beautify his wife by helping her grow more into the likeness of Christ. But human love is not, or perhaps is only very rarely, beautifying at its outset. I do not know anyone who has begun to love someone while finding him or her positively lacking in the principal kinds of beauty. Most relationships probably begin with each party being aware of things that might happily be changed in the other, but a preponderance of such sentiment will spell trouble for the future. Human beings conceive a romantic love for those they find beautiful in some way. The characters we have already met illustrate this: the elders of Troy describe Helen as 'fearfully like the immortal goddesses to look at'.[1]

---

1. Homer, *The Iliad*, tr. Martin Hammond (Harmondsworth: Penguin, 1987), p. 45.

Romeo says that Juliet has 'Beauty too rich for use, for earth too dear.'[2] Zuleika's visage, though not classically beautiful, 'bewitched' the Duke of Dorset instantly.[3]

God loves the unlovely

By contrast, God loves us when we are unlovely to him. He finds us languishing in the filth of our sin and chooses to cleanse and make us holy. Samuel Crossman expresses this idea beautifully in his hymn:

> Love to the loveless shown,
> That they might lovely be.

Christ is a husband who makes the church beautiful when he weds her, not a husband who wants to wed her because she is beautiful. Martin Luther put the contrast between divine and human love very well in his twenty-eighth thesis for the Heidelberg Disputation in 1518: 'The love of God does not find, but creates, that which is pleasing to it. The love of man comes into being through that which is pleasing to it.'[4]

Paul teaches in Ephesians 1:4 that God gives his people the beauty of holiness: 'he chose us in him before the foundation of the world, that we should be holy and blameless before him'. Note the wording: 'should be', not 'because we were'. God's love is a holiness-creating love, not a holiness-finding love. In Christ God creates the beauty of those he loves:

> Christ loved the church and gave himself up for her, that he might sanctify her, having cleansed her by the washing of water with the

---

2. William Shakespeare, *Romeo and Juliet*, ed. René Weis (London: Bloomsbury, 2012; repr. 2013), I. v. 46, p. 171.

3. Max Beerbohm, *Zuleika Dobson* (London: Minerva, 1991), p. 18.

4. Martin Luther, *Martin Luther's Basic Theological Writings*, ed. Timothy F. Lull (Minneapolis: Fortress, 1989), p. 32.

word, so that he might present the church to himself in splendour, without spot or wrinkle or any such thing, that she might be holy and without blemish. (Eph. 5:25–27)

Note the connection here between Ephesians 1 and 5: in chapter 1 Paul praises God for choosing the church to be holy, and in chapter 5 he writes of Christ the bridegroom dying in history to make the church holy. As C. S. Lewis writes, 'the Church has no beauty but what the Bridegroom gives her; he does not find, but makes her, lovely'.[5] In eternity God chose us to be holy and in time Christ makes us holy. The cross is God's revelation in time of his purpose in eternity. Why is this his purpose? Why does God love us if he does not find us beautiful? Quite simply, because this is who he is, as Leon Morris explains: 'He loves not because of what we are, but because of what he is: he *is* love.'[6]

Our thinking can be so warped that we find this good news hard to accept. While we ought to delight in being beautified, we all too easily grumble about being told that we are not beautiful by ourselves. We are like a bride whose beauty on her wedding day is accentuated by her dress and the glorious tresses in her hair, but who finds in people's compliments only an insult to her previous appearance: 'What was wrong with how I looked before?' John Calvin saw how 'we always desire to be somewhat, and such is our folly, we even think we are'.[7] Lewis also notes how we struggle to remember our place:

Depth beneath depth and subtlety within subtlety, there remains some lingering idea of our own, our very own, attractiveness. It is easy to acknowledge, but almost impossible to realise for long, that we are mirrors whose brightness, if we are bright, is wholly derived from the

5. C. S. Lewis, *The Four Loves* (London: Collins, 1963; repr. 1965), p. 97.

6. Leon Morris, *Testaments of Love: A Study of Love in the Bible* (Grand Rapids: Eerdmans, 1981), p. 142 (italics original).

7. John Calvin, *Canons and Decrees of the Council of Trent, with the Antidote*, in Henry Beveridge (ed. and tr.), *Selected Works of John Calvin: Tracts and Letters*, 7 vols. (Edinburgh: Calvin Translation Society, 1851; repr. Grand Rapids: Baker Book House, 1983), 3.108.

sun that shines upon us. Surely we must have a little – however little –
native luminosity? Surely we can't be *quite* creatures?[8]

Certainly it is humbling to acknowledge that we are not by nature
beautiful, but we must not forget that it is astounding good news
that God makes us beautiful! It is the good news of the gospel. It
is the good news of who God is.

Ezekiel's Jerusalem

Among all the passages of the Bible this is perhaps most vividly
displayed in Ezekiel 16, where God tells the story of his dealings with
Jerusalem. Why did God save Jerusalem? Was it because he found
her beautiful? The prophet gives a shocking answer. God found Israel
filthy, with nothing attractive in her. She was like a victim of infanti-
cide, a baby girl born to pagan parents and discarded in a field with
the umbilical cord still not cut from the placenta. Unwashed, unloved,
cast out, abhorred, she was left wallowing in her own blood. It was
God who rescued her, who gave her life and growth, and then
adorned her with embroidered cloth, fine linen, silk, jewellery, a
crown and royal dignity. Her famous beauty, seen most obviously in
the visit of the Queen of Sheba to Solomon, was not natural to her
but bestowed by God: 'your renown went forth among the nations
because of your beauty, for it was perfect through the splendour that
I had bestowed on you' (v. 14).

God's dealings with Jerusalem here are an epitome of his dealings
with Israel, and his dealings with Israel are a microcosm of his
dealings with the world. Israel stands as a new Adam, the new
humanity, the beginning of God's rescue plan for the world. The
way in which he saves Israel is a type of the way in which he saves
the church. Some aspects of Israel's life are unique to her, but the
theme of her helplessness and lack of beauty is one that is carried
through into the New Testament and must be applied to the people
of God in all times.

---

8. Lewis, *Four Loves*, pp. 119–120 (italics original).

There are also reminders in Ezekiel 16 of themes I have explored in earlier chapters. Note the emphasis on God's sovereign love. He takes the initiative, giving life to Jerusalem by his word 'Live!', just as he made Adam live at the beginning (v. 6). He spreads the corner of his garment over her and initiates his marriage covenant with her (v. 8). Observe too how his love does not change, despite Jerusalem's ugly rebellion. The prophet tells of how the city trusted in her own beauty and played the whore (v. 15), only she paid her lovers rather than taking money from them (vv. 33–34). She made idols out of her jewels and even sacrificed her own children to them (vv. 17–21). As a result of her sin, the Lord warns that he will bring upon her 'the blood of wrath and jealousy' (v. 38). The very nations she has loved will strip, stone and dismember her (vv. 39–40). Nevertheless God's love will remain upon her. Later in the chapter he affirms his unchanging purpose: 'yet I will remember my covenant with you in the days of your youth, and I will establish for you an everlasting covenant' (v. 60).

God's love of benevolence and complaisance

The striking imagery of Ezekiel 16 highlights the wonder of God's beautifying love, but we may feel that such love has troubling implications. Does it mean that God does not have any delight in us as we are in ourselves? If God's love confers beauty, does he never actually love me as I am, for whatever beauty I have? The Puritan writers can help us here. They often employ a distinction between God's love of benevolence and his love of complaisance. These unusual words denote something quite simple. A love of benevolence is a good-bestowing love, a love that confers some good thing on its object. By contrast, a love of complaisance is a good-finding love, a love that finds something already in its object and delights in it.

God clearly has a love of benevolence for fallen creatures. It was benevolent love when he said to Jerusalem 'Live!' and when he adorned her with fine clothes and jewellery, royal dignity and renown. All of this was his loving, good-bestowing action towards his people. The same is true of us today. When God chose us for holiness before

1) don't see people as 3mag 'siull Part, non-Siull Part :

the creation of the world, it was an act of benevolent love, a holiness-bestowing love, not a holiness-finding love.

Does this mean that God never has a love of complaisance for us, that he never delights in us as we are in our fallen condition? It does not, because God loves the remnant of his own image in us. In so far as we are his creatures, made by him and sustained by him, even the worst of us contains this remnant. As I explained in chapter 1, the image of God is ruined but not entirely erased by the fall (Gen. 5:1–3; 9:6; Jas 3:9). All created things retain some good, and evil is a deficiency rather than a created thing itself. God alone creates. The devil does not create; he can only twist and pervert what God has made. Augustine explains that 'evil has no existence except as a privation of good'.[9] So everything that exists has a remnant of good in it since it has the good of existence. This much must follow from the Bible's doctrine of creation. In that good remnant, God delights with a love of complaisance.

My concern here is not, however, with the general complaisance of God in the vestiges of goodness that remain in a fallen world, but with his saving love for his people, the love that he made manifest in sending his Son so that we might live (1 John 4:8–9). The question is not whether God has some delight even in fallen creatures, but whether such delight explains his decision to save. No doubt when God saves, he delights to restore the remnant of his image in us, but why does he save in the first place? Does he do so impelled by the remnant of beauty in us, or does he do so to create beauty?

God hates the sin, and hates the sinner

The Bible's answer is unmistakable: as fallen image bearers we are full of sin and under God's wrath. We are 'children of wrath' (Eph. 2:3). God does not save us because he delights in us in our fallen condition. If God's saving love were impelled by the remnant of goodness in us, then he would save everyone, even the demons, since

---

9. Augustine, *Confessions*, tr. Henry Chadwick (Oxford: Oxford University Press, 1992), 3.7, p. 43.

all have some remnant of goodness. But he does not save all, even of the human race. The Bible is full of testimony not to God's delight in fallen creatures impelling him to save, but to his hatred for sin.

Moreover, we cannot say that God saves because he hates only our sin and not us. The Bible goes even further than speaking of God's hatred for sin: it states that God hates the sinner. God's hatred is not a spiteful, capricious malevolence. Rather, it is the implacable reaction of his perfectly holy being to evil. But it is directed at sinners who sin and not abstractly at their sin apart from them. We cannot seek refuge in the epithet that 'God hates the sin but loves the sinner'. That is a memorable way of trying to express how God reacts against sin and yet still loves his creatures, but it relies on an unsustainable distinction between the sin and the sinner. It is true that in passages such as Romans 6 – 7 sin is personified, but it never exists apart from a sinner. When God hates sin, he is hating the thoughts and actions of sinners. When I commit a sin, it is not something that can be separated from me, as if it does not affect who I am.

We need to grasp the connection between our acts and our being. I am more than what I do, but what I do affects who I am. Alan Torrance expresses the weakness of the epithet well:

> The problem with this statement is that it falsely separates our sin and our alienation from our *being*. Our sins become extrinsic to our being. But this reflects a failure to appreciate the nature of sin. Sin is not ontologically insignificant or incidental. It denotes what we *are*, that is, our 'being-in-act' and our whole orientation – our 'minds.' We are not essentially God's lovable friends and hostile only in our extrinsic acts.[10]

If I sin, then I become a sinner, and God hates me because the sin is mine, as Scripture explicitly states:

---

10. 'Is Love the Essence of God?', in Kevin J. Vanhoozer (ed.), *Nothing Greater, Nothing Better: Theological Essays on the Love of God* (Grand Rapids: Eerdmans, 2001), p. 132, n. 33 (italics original).

You are not a God who delights in wickedness;
    evil may not dwell with you.
The boastful shall not stand before your eyes;
    you hate all evildoers.
(Ps. 5:4–5)

Or again:

The LORD tests the righteous,
    but his soul hates the wicked and the one who loves violence.
(Ps. 11:5)

John himself writes of God's wrath remaining on 'whoever does not obey the Son' (John 3:36).

When God loves us, he does not love us because he finds our real self lovable, as if sin is something only on the periphery of our being and we are really quite lovely on the inside. God finds us permeated by sin, and yet still loves us. His saving love is not, therefore, to be explained as a delight in who we really are in our inward selves. Indeed, if we do think that God hates sin as something separate from us but loves us as we really are, then we actually reduce the wonder of his love because we end up deserving it deep down. It is far more astonishing that the God who hates us as sinners nonetheless, despite our sinfulness and with it in full view, sets his love upon us.

God delights in us

How then can we say that God sets his love upon us if he hates us? If God hates our sin and hates us as sinners, then how does he also love us with delight? Should we conclude that God simply does not have any delight in us, that his saving love is only a love of benevolence and never complaisance?

We can address this question by asking a slightly different one and then working our way back to it. The question we begin with is this: Is there anywhere in creation a loveliness in which God delights without reserve? Is there one for whom he has an unalloyed love of complaisance, one in whom he might find what is lovely and take unqualified delight in it?

Surely there is: his own Son, our saviour the Lord Jesus Christ. When the Father loves the Son, he delights in the radiance of his own glory and the exact representation of his being (Heb. 1:3). As the Lord Jesus begins his public ministry, the Father announces that he delights in him: 'This is my beloved Son, with whom I am well pleased' (Matt. 3:17). Jesus is the one sinless man in whom God the Father rejoices without reserve. Most of all, the Father delights in the obedience of his Son as he goes to death, even death on a cross: 'For this reason the Father loves me, because I lay down my life that I may take it up again' (John 10:17). The Son is the one the Father loves with a love of unreserved complaisance.

How does this help us with our question about the nature of God's saving love for us? Here is the amazing thing: the Father delights in the Son, so that when we are included in Christ, he delights in us too. How does this happen? It is because we are *in* and *with* Christ. John uses the image of the vine and the branches (John 15:5); Paul teaches that our union with Christ was decreed before the creation of the world (Eph. 1:4) and that our lives are now hidden with Christ in God (Col. 3:3). All that we are as Christians we are because of our spiritual union with Christ.

God does not save us because he finds us lovely in ourselves and takes complaisant delight in us. He does have a complaisant love for his own image in us, but that is not why he saves us. Plainly as fallen people we do not deserve to be saved on the basis of the remnant image in us. Yet God saves not only because he is benevolent to us, but because he is also complaisant in us *in Christ*. He delights in us not as he finds us bloody and dead in sin, but as he relates to us in Christ. Regarding us in Christ, decreed from eternity, united to him by the Spirit in our regeneration, living day by day rooted in him, abiding for ever in him, God delights in us. God saves us because of Jesus, and he loves us with total complaisance because he delights in him.

But does he really love *me*?

Perhaps you still find this unsatisfying? Do you wonder if it means that God does not love you as you really are? That he does not actually delight in you, but only in Jesus? Perhaps even that he does not delight in the *real* you, the sinful you, but only in the unreal you 'in Christ'? In his classic *Agape and Eros* the Swedish theologian Anders Nygren follows Luther by insisting strongly that God's love does not respond to our merit or worth.[11] Gary Badcock objects that on Nygren's view 'God does not love *them*, after all, for who they are and what they are'. It seems as if God 'agrees with the pathological self-image of the depressed person'.[12]

It is striking that Badcock meets Nygren's moral argument about human demerit with a psychological response, reflecting the preference of our age for the language of feelings rather than rights and wrongs. That aside, the first deeper problem with such thinking is that it fails to grasp the depth of human depravity. A negative *moral* self-image is not a pathological condition, but a true estimate of our standing as sinners before the holy God. There are mistaken kinds of low self-esteem that wrongly trouble us, but the answer to those is not to inflate our estimate of how we deserve the love of God.

The second problem is that such thinking has not grasped the significance of the recreation of the Christian in Christ. Because of the gospel, depressed people can have a rightly bleak estimate of themselves outside Christ and at the same time rejoice in what God has now made them in Christ. To think that the real you is the sinful you is to fall for a cruel lie of Satan. The real you is not the sin-ridden old self but the new you in Christ. All of your sin is a remnant of the old self. It is the flesh. It will be with you till you die. But it is not the real you. It has been decisively crucified, put to death. The real you is you in Christ: 'you have died, and your life is hidden with

---

11. On this central point Nygren was absolutely right, but his schematized approach to the vocabulary of love was flawed, as D. A. Carson succinctly shows in *The Difficult Doctrine of the Love of God* (Wheaton: Crossway; Leicester: Inter-Varsity Press, 2000), pp. 25–28.

12. Gary D. Badcock, 'The Concept of Love: Divine and Human', in Kevin J. Vanhoozer (ed.), *Nothing Greater, Nothing Better: Theological Essays on the Love of God* (Grand Rapids: Eerdmans, 2001), p. 36 (italics original).

Christ in God' (Col. 3:3). Your life in Christ is not your less real life. God has decided who you are in Christ.

The devil lies to us about who we are, desperately tempting us to return to his shadow reality, to accept his word about ourselves and to despair. He dredges up our old sins and parades them before us, telling us that this is who we are, that God cannot possibly love us. But God's Word is true, and he has declared us to be new creatures in Christ. This is no legal fiction, as if God pretends we are new people in Christ. To identify us with Christ, God uproots us from Adam and plants us in Christ, our head in the covenant of grace. He does not simply decide to treat us as if we were in Christ, but binds us to him by filling us with his Spirit. Christ is our legal representative, standing for us in our relationship with his Father, but he is also the head of the church, to whom we his body are organically united by his Spirit. We really are in Christ, and God delights in us in him, as we truly are.

Meditation

Thomas Goodwin describes how the apostle Paul in Romans 5 and 1 Corinthians 15 tells the story of Adam and Christ 'as if there had never been any more men in the world, nor were ever to be for time to come, except these two'. Why does Paul sum up the history of the race like this? Goodwin explains that it is because 'these two between them had all the rest of the sons of men hanging at their girdle'. Edward Donnelly strikingly takes up and develops Goodwin's picture and invites us to dwell on our new identity in Christ:

> Can you visualize the picture which Goodwin draws for us? He imagines two great giants, one called Adam and the other Christ. Each is wearing an enormous leather 'girdle' or belt with millions of little hooks on it. You and I, and all humanity, are hanging either at Adam's belt or at Christ's belt. There is no third option, no other place for us. And God deals with us only through Adam or through Christ. If you are hanging at Adam's belt, you share in the experience of sinful, fallen Adam, and your entire relationship with God is through him. But if you are hanging at Christ's belt, all God's dealings with you are through Christ. When you

received Jesus as your Saviour, you were involved in a massive and momentous transfer. The Almighty himself unhooked you from Adam's belt and hooked you on to Christ's. So you now have a different Head, a different Mediator, a new Representative. You have passed from Adam into Christ, and whereas God formerly dealt with you only through Adam, he now deals with you only through his Son. You are in Christ unchangeably and for ever.[13]

- *Visualize the two giant figures and yourself hanging from the belt of the old Adam.*

- *Now see yourself being lifted by the hand of God and hooked onto Christ, never to be removed.*

Consider for a moment the fact that God delights in you with the love he has for his Son in whom you are loved. God the Father loves the Son from and for all eternity. He loves him perfectly, completely, with an immortal love. He delights in him with an infinite delight. You are recreated in Christ. God has plucked you out of Adam and made you a new creation in his Son. This means that the Father loves you with the same perfect, complete, immortal love he has for his Son. He delights in you with the same infinite delight he has for Christ. Love pours eternally between the persons of the Holy Trinity so that God's very being is an eternal fountain of love. You are loved within that love, bathed in that flow. God looks at you and 'delights' in you (Isa. 62:4).

- *Consider the delightfulness of the Son to the Father, the Father's love for the Son, and yourself enveloped within it.*

The beautifying love of God summons us to the utter renunciation of all delusions of spiritual grandeur. We are not born beautiful. God finds us naked and wallowing in our own bloody mess. All beauty that we have, we have from him. His the clothing! His the

---

13. Edward Donnelly, *Biblical Teaching on the Doctrines of Heaven and Hell* (Edinburgh: Banner of Truth Trust, 2001; repr. 2005), p. 87–88.

jewellery! His the crown! His the renown! We can but ask ourselves what Paul asked the Corinthian Christians: 'What do you have that you did not receive? If then you received it, why do you boast as if you did not receive it?' (1 Cor. 4:7). Let us fall awed before the throne of God, dumbstruck as we grasp afresh our old abject spiritual ugliness and our new stunning beauty in the Son of God.

- *Consider yourself as you would be outside Christ.*

- *Now reflect on what it means for you to be hidden with Christ in God.*

Prayer

'Heavenly Father, you found me cast off in a pool of blood. I was naked and unloved. And yet you picked me up. You commanded me to live. You clothed me. You took me as your bride. You adorned me with the jewels of your Son. You made me beautiful in him. I stand perfect in your sight because you have enfolded me in his beauty, given him my filth and wrapped me in his obedience. I praise you for your kindness to me in Jesus. I marvel to find myself loved with your love for him, an overflowing, eternal, perfect love.

'Keep me from unfaithfulness. Do not let me trust in my beauty as if it were my own. Keep me always conscious that I am by nature a sinner deserving your hatred.

'Remind me that I am loved because I am in your Son Jesus, and that I am truly who I am in him. Protect me from the lie of Satan who whispers in my ear that the true me is the old me. Help me to see myself as you see me in your Son. Keep me always trusting in him, that I might be part of his bride when she appears, adorned and ready for him. In his name. Amen.'

CONCLUSION

We live in a love-obsessed age. In such an environment it is tempting for us to reject the world's obsession with love, to scorn the songs and books and films, to search for something else at the centre of the Christian faith that will distinguish us from this love craze. I trust that by now it will be clear that such a search would prove fruitless, because love *is* at the heart of the gospel, and of the being of God himself. The answer for a Christian living in a love-mad culture is not to repudiate any interest in love, but to subvert it with the truth.

This is what God did when Israel succumbed to the pagan idolatry of love and sex that surrounded her. Through the prophet Hosea God attacks the 'whoring' of the Israelites (Hos. 2:2). He does not, however, reject the language or imagery of love. In fact he develops it to new levels, describing his redemptive work as a marriage, picturing Israel once again calling him 'My Husband' (2:16), and giving her the great promise 'I will betroth you to me in righteousness and in justice, in steadfast love and in mercy' (2:19). As David Hubbard states, 'Hosea's answer to the harlotry with the Baals was not a prudish rejection of the love relationship but an absolute claim to it.'[1] Rather than rejecting the terms of the debate, 'Yahweh played

---

1. David Allan Hubbard, *Hosea: An Introduction and Commentary* (Leicester: Inter-Varsity Press, 1989), p. 29.

Baal on his own court and demonstrated who was the more faithful, the truly loving Lover.'[2]

God's subversion of the Baals' claim to be the true lover of his people reaches its zenith when he even appears to take on his own lips the names of the Canaanite gods:

> O Ephraim, what have I to do with idols?
>> It is I who answer and look after you.
>
> (Hos. 14:8)

In the Hebrew the word for 'answering' (*'ănîtî*) sounds like the name of the Canaanite god Anat, and the word for 'looking after' (*wa'ăšûrennû*) sounds like the god Asherah. In just a few astonishing words God manages to distance himself from the idols and to subvert their claims. For some commentators this interpretation is just too much to stomach, especially since God had said he would make Israel forget the names of the gods (Hos. 2:17).[3] But the way in which he would make them forget their false gods was not by erasing everything they had sought for in the Baals. Rather, all the good things Israel wrongly looked for under the names of the gods would be found in Yahweh alone. Their very names were transformed into the shape of verbs describing what he alone would do for them. God is the true husband of his people.

The church holds out to a love-obsessed culture true love, the love of God. What is that love like? I have described how it is different from human love and infinitely greater than it. God's love is, in the words of Samuel Francis's hymn, the 'love of every love the best'. When we love, we may feel that we must be the first ever to have had this amazing intensity of experience, but before any creature ever loved, God is love. We may love with an extraordinary devotion, to the point of turning what we love into an idol and hurting it, but God's love is always rightly proportioned. We live in a time when fatherhood is breaking down, but God is the perfect Father who makes us his children and promises never to leave us. We love because

---

2. Ibid., pp. 29–30.

3. So ibid., pp. 232–233, n. 1.

we need to love, but God loves without any need for his beloved, purely from the overflow of his goodness. Our force of affection may leave us helpless before one we love, but God is always sovereign in his love. Our love may wax and wane, but God loves with an eternal and unchanging love. Our passion varies, but God loves with a passion full of the highest degree of life. The more we discover about someone, the harder it may be to love them, but God knows us perfectly from the outset and still loves us. We may harbour a desire for retribution that destroys our love, but God forgives us and at the same time maintains the demand of his own holy being for justice. We may seek a beautiful bride, but God finds us in the filth of sin and lifts us up, washes us, clothes us and makes us beautiful. In these ways and many more God's love is different from our love in its manner, and the uniqueness of its manner lends it a peerless magnitude.

I have tried to offer you a glimpse of the love of God from the Scriptures in this book. I am thrilled by what we have seen, but as I draw to a close my attempt feels flimsy and inadequate against the reality, this book like fragments of crumbling paper scattered by a mighty wind. This majestic, glorious, unfathomable divine love will be our inexhaustible eternal occupation. We are teetering only on the brink of edging across the margins of the very beginning of understanding it. Even so, for now the love of God is to be lived as well as learned. So as you close this book and return to human company, I offer you the gentle reminder that 'love begets love'.[4] May the word abide in us, and may it not return empty as, by miracles of grace, we make this love visible in our lives.

---

4. A quotation from Leon Morris, *Testaments of Love: A Study of Love in the Bible* (Grand Rapids: Eerdmans, 1981), p. 277.

BIBLIOGRAPHY

Abelard and Heloise, *The Letters and Other Writings*, ed. and tr. William
    Levitan (Indianapolis: Hackett, 2007).

Appleyard, Brain, 'Distraction', *The Sunday Times*, 20 July 2008, http://
    bryanappleyard.com/distraction (accessed 4 Nov. 2014).

Augustine, *Confessions*, tr. Henry Chadwick (Oxford: Oxford University
    Press, 1992).

Badcock, Gary D., 'The Concept of Love: Divine and Human', in Kevin
    J. Vanhoozer (ed.), *Nothing Greater, Nothing Better: Theological Essays on
    the Love of God* (Grand Rapids: Eerdmans, 2001), pp. 30–46.

Bavinck, Herman, *Our Reasonable Faith*, tr. Henry Zylstra (Grand Rapids:
    Eerdmans, 1956).

Beerbohm, Max, *Zuleika Dobson* (London: Minerva, 1991).

Boethius, *The Consolation of Philosophy*, tr. S. J. Tester, in *Boethius*, Loeb
    Classical Library 74 (Cambridge, Mass.: Harvard University Press;
    London: William Heinemann, 1973; repr. 1978).

Bonar, Andrew, *Memoir and Remains of the Rev. Robert Murray M'Cheyne*,
    2nd ed. (Dundee: William Middleton, 1852).

Calvin, John, *Canons and Decrees of the Council of Trent, with the Antidote*, in
    Henry Beveridge (ed. and tr.), *Selected Works of John Calvin: Tracts and
    Letters*, 7 vols. (Edinburgh: Calvin Translation Society, 1851; repr. Grand
    Rapids: Baker Book House, 1983), vol. 3.

————, *Institutes of the Christian Religion*, ed. John T. McNeill, tr. Ford Lewis
    Battles, 2 vols., Library of Christian Classics 20–21 (Philadelphia:
    Westminster, 1960).

————, *Selected Works of John Calvin: Tracts and Letters*, ed. Henry Beveridge
    and Jules Bonnet (Grand Rapids: Baker Book House, 1983).

Carson, D. A., *The Difficult Doctrine of the Love of God* (Wheaton: Crossway;
    Leicester: Inter-Varsity Press, 2000).

Chalke, Steve, 'Cross Purposes', *Christianity*, Sept. 2004, pp. 44–48.

Charnock, Stephen, *The Existence and Attributes of God* (Grand Rapids: Baker,
    1996; repr. 2000).

Dennis, Norman, 'Beautiful Theories, Brutal Facts: The Welfare State and
    Sexual Liberation', in David Smith (ed.), *Welfare, Work and Poverty: Lessons
    from Recent Reforms in the USA and the UK* (London: Institute for the Study
    of Civil Society, 2000), pp. 45–80.

Dennis, Norman, and George Erdos, *Families Without Fatherhood*, 3rd ed.
    (London: Institute for the Study of Civil Society, 2000).

Donnelly, Edward, *Biblical Teaching on the Doctrines of Heaven and Hell*
    (Edinburgh: Banner of Truth Trust, 2001; repr. 2005).

Edwards, Jonathan, *The Nature of True Virtue*, ed. Paul Ramsey, in John E.
    Smith (ed.), *The Works of Jonathan Edwards* (New Haven: Yale University
    Press, 1989), vol. 8.

Ferguson, Sinclair B., *Children of the Living God* (Edinburgh: Banner of Truth
    Trust, 1989; repr. 2011).

Gillespie, Patrick, *The Ark of the Covenant Opened: Or, A Treatise of the Covenant
    of Redemption* (London: Thomas Parkhurst, 1677).

Gilson, Étienne, *Abelard and Heloise*, tr. L. K. Shook (Ann Arbor: University
    of Michigan Press, 1960).

Gregory the Great, *Morals on the Book of Job*, ed. Paul A. Böer, 3 vols. (n.p.:
    Veritatis Splendor, 2012).

Hanks, Patrick, Kate Hardcastle and Flavia Hodges, *A Dictionary of First
    Names*, 2nd ed. (Oxford: Oxford University Press, 2006).

Hare, Robert D., *Without Conscience: The Disturbing World of the Psychopaths
    Among Us* (New York: Guildford, 1999).

Hart, Trevor, 'How Do We Define the Nature of God's Love?', in Kevin
    J. Vanhoozer (ed.), *Nothing Greater, Nothing Better: Theological Essays on
    the Love of God* (Grand Rapids: Eerdmans, 2001), pp. 94–113.

Hilary of Poitiers, *On the Trinity*, in Philip Schaff and Henry Wace (eds.),
    Nicene and Post-Nicene Fathers, second series, 14 vols. (Buffalo:

Christian Literature, 1886–90; repr. Peabody: Hendrickson, 1994), vol. 9.

Homer, *The Iliad*, tr. Martin Hammond (Harmondsworth: Penguin, 1987).

Hubbard, David Allan, *Hosea: An Introduction and Commentary* (Leicester: Inter-Varsity Press, 1989).

James, Henry, *The Art of Criticism: Henry James on the Theory and the Practice of Fiction*, ed. William Veeder and Susan M. Griffin (Chicago: University of Chicago Press, 1986).

The Koran: Interpreted, tr. Arthur J. Arberry (Oxford: Oxford University Press, 1983; repr. 2008).

Lactantius, *The Divine Institutes*, in Alexander Roberts and James Donaldson (eds.), *Ante-Nicene Fathers*, 10 vols. (Buffalo: Christian Literature, 1885–96; repr. Peabody: Hendrickson, 1995), vol. 7.

——, *A Treatise on the Anger of God*, in Philip Schaff (ed.), *Nicene and Post-Nicene Fathers*, first series, 14 vols. (Buffalo: Christian Literature, 1886–90; repr. Peabody: Hendrickson, 1994), vol. 7.

Lewis, C. S., *The Four Loves* (London: Collins, 1963; repr. 1965).

——, 'On the Reading of Old Books', in Walter Hooper (ed.), *God in the Dock* (Grand Rapids: Eerdmans, 2014), pp. 217–225.

Luther, Martin, *Martin Luther's Basic Theological Writings*, ed. Timothy F. Lull (Minneapolis: Fortress, 1989).

Machen, J. Gresham, *Christianity and Liberalism* (Grand Rapids: Eerdmans, 2009).

Milton, John, *Paradise Lost*, ed. John Leonard (London: Penguin, 2000).

Moltmann, Jürgen, *The Crucified God: The Cross of Christ as the Foundation and Criticism of Christian Theology*, tr. R. A. Wilson and John Bowden (Minneapolis: Fortress, 1993).

Moore, Suzanne, 'Yes, Divorce Is Bad for Children, but Let's Not Fetishise Marriage at All Costs', *The Guardian*, 24 Nov. 2014.

Morris, Leon, *Testaments of Love: A Study of Love in the Bible* (Grand Rapids: Eerdmans, 1981).

Murray, John, *Redemption Accomplished and Applied* (Edinburgh: Banner of Truth Trust, 1961).

O'Brien, Peter T., *The Letter to the Hebrews* (Grand Rapids: Eerdmans; Nottingham: Apollos, 2010).

Owen, John, *The Death of Death in the Death of Christ*, in William H. Goold (ed.), *The Works of John Owen*, 16 vols. (Edinburgh: Banner of Truth Trust, 1965–8; repr. 1993), vol. 10.

————, *A Dissertation on Divine Justice*, in William H. Goold (ed.), *The Works of John Owen*, 16 vols. (Edinburgh: Banner of Truth Trust, 1965–8; repr. 1993), vol. 10.

'Parole Denied in School Shooting', *USA Today*, 19 June 2001, http://www. usatoday.com/news/nation/2001-04-18-spencer.htm (accessed 25 July 2012).

Piper, John, 'Are There Two Wills in God?', in Thomas R. Schreiner and Bruce A. Ware (eds.), *Still Sovereign: Contemporary Perspectives on Election, Foreknowledge, and Grace* (Grand Rapids: Baker, 2000), pp. 107–131.

Plato, *The Symposium*, tr. Walter Hamilton (London: Penguin, 1951).

Regoli, Robert M., John D. Hewitt and Matt DeLisi, *Delinquency in Society*, 8th ed. (Sudbury, Mass.: Jones & Bartlett, 2010).

Rosner, Brian S., '"Known by God": The Meaning and Value of a Neglected Biblical Concept', *Tyndale Bulletin* 59.2 (2008), pp. 207–230.

Shakespeare, William, *Romeo and Juliet*, ed. René Weis (London: Bloomsbury, 2012; repr. 2013).

'Statistical Bulletin: Divorces in England and Wales 2010: Children of Divorced Couples', *Office for National Statistics*, http://www.ons.gov.uk/ ons/rel/vsob1/divorces-in-england-and-wales/2010/stb-divorces-2010. html#tab-children-of-divorced-couples (accessed 13 Aug. 2012).

'Statistical Bulletin: Divorces in England and Wales 2010: Duration of Marriage', *Office for National Statistics*, http://www.ons.gov.uk/ons/rel/ vsob1/divorces-in-england-and-wales/2010/stb-divorces-2010. html#tab-duration-of-marriage (accessed 13 Aug. 2012).

'Statistical Bulletin: Divorces in England and Wales 2010: Summary', *Office for National Statistics*, http://www.ons.gov.uk/ons/rel/vsob1/divorces-in-england-and-wales/2010/stb-divorces-2010.html (accessed 13 Aug. 2012).

'Supporting Families', *The National Archives*, http://webarchive. nationalarchives.gov.uk/+/http:/www.nationalarchives.gov.uk/ erorecords/ho/421/2/p2/acu/suppfam.htm#foreword (accessed 20 Nov. 2014).

Torrance, Alan J., 'Is Love the Essence of God?', in Kevin J. Vanhoozer (ed.), *Nothing Greater, Nothing Better: Theological Essays on the Love of God* (Grand Rapids: Eerdmans, 2001), pp. 114–137.

Turretin, Francis, *Institutes of Elenctic Theology*, ed. James T. Dennison, tr. George Musgrave Giger, 3 vols. (Phillipsburg: P. & R., 1992–7).

Tyrrell, George, *Christianity at the Cross-Roads* (London: Longmans, Green, 1910).

Vanhoozer, Kevin J., 'Introduction: The Love of God – Its Place, Meaning, and Function in Systematic Theology', in Kevin J. Vanhoozer (ed.), *Nothing Greater, Nothing Better: Theological Essays on the Love of God* (Grand Rapids: Eerdmans, 2001), pp. 1–29.

Wells, David F., *God in the Whirlwind: How the Holy Love of God Reorients Our World* (Nottingham: Inter-Varsity Press, 2014).

Wilson, Douglas J., *Reforming Marriage*, 2nd ed. (Moscow, Idaho: Canon, 2005).

INDEX OF SCRIPTURE REFERENCES

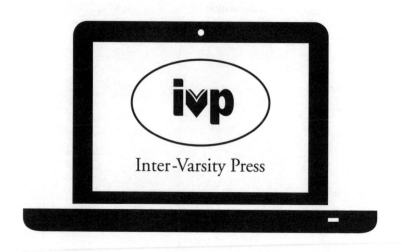

Inter-Varsity Press

For more information about IVP
and our publications visit

www.ivpbooks.com

Get regular updates at **ivpbooks.com/signup**
Find us on **facebook.com/ivpbooks**
Follow us on **twitter.com/ivpbookcentre**

Inter-Varsity Press, a company limited by guarantee registered in England and Wales, number 05202650. Registered
office IVP Bookcentre, Norton Street, Nottingham NG7 3HR, United Kingdom. Registered charity number 1105757.